Blueprint For Marriage

Marriage by Design

Gary Overholt

ISBN: 978-1-365-83766-1

PublishNation LLC
www.publishnation.net

Contents

Acknowledgments

I would like to give special thanks to my lovely wife, Fran, who helped me develop this material through the course of many years of tirelessly teaching, mentoring and helping hundreds of couples. It has truly been an extraordinary experience working so closely with her, an experience that most pastor-teachers only dream of.

I would also like to thank my three sons, Carl, Casey and Cary, who are godly men, husbands and fathers, who validate my own ministry through their lifestyles.

And special thanks to my brother Walt, who volunteered his time and talent in helping me critique this work.

1

Why Do We Need a Blueprint?

The best stuff always comes from some sort of blueprint. When I was a kid, I loved to race around with my friends in old cars. We would save our money to buy high performance parts for our old jalopies and then take them out to secluded spots to illegally drag race them. We would dream about having cars with real muscle, but most of the time, we just drove mediocre cars that sounded fast and needed fixing. My dream car was a 1967 Chevrolet Camaro Z28 with a blueprinted 302 racing engine. Back then, we talked about blueprinted engines because everybody knew they were the coolest and fastest way to go. Precision machining was the key, but that couldn't be accomplished without a blueprint. I never did get my dream car, but I did get my dream marriage by following God's blueprint design for marriage.

If you are struggling in your marriage or just want a better marriage, let me encourage you to go high performance. Go with a blueprint. With cars and houses, there are many blueprints to choose from, but when it comes to marriage, most of us just build as we go on the assumption that we know enough to make it work. The build-as-you-go plan never seemed to work out too well for me and my drag racing buddies. We blew more parts and money without a plan and really never went all that fast. The best blueprint for marriage comes from the original designer, God. We find his blueprint rolled up in the pages of the Bible. What do you have to lose? When all else fails, follow the directions, or in this case the blueprint. A lot of very wise information comes from some really old books. Old-book knowledge has usually been time tested, it usually gives us a perspective that oft times has been lost or ignored by modern man, and what goes around comes around: old-book knowledge is the key to new discoveries, especially when it comes to human relationships. Why do we spend so much money on libraries and data banks?

Useful knowledge is sometimes lost and needs to be rediscovered. Even if you're not very religious or even believe in God, you might just benefit from following the wise old blueprint for marriage found in the pages of the Bible instead of the haphazard build as you go modern version.

Following a Blueprint

Think about a set of blueprints. They are very precise yet creative, something engineered to specifications, yet drawn like art. Blueprints represent the ultimate expression of professional creativity and depending on the skill set of the person who creates them, with their intelligence, knowledge, skill, and intuitive ability, blueprints become a tool that can help virtually anybody who knows how to read them. Blueprints help re-create what the designer intended. A design can be very complex or extremely simple, but in either case, the blueprint is a tool that can be used to re-create what somebody else has envisioned in his or her mind. When the designer and builder are one and the same, the end result is assured. In the case of marriage, we must ask the questions: "Do we have a designer, and if we have a designer of marriage, did that designer have a purpose in mind, and did that purposeful design come with a blueprint?" The fact of the matter is the Bible does reveal for us a blueprint for marriage. It is a very simple blueprint, but at the same time, very precise. When the designer of a set of plans has a goal or purpose in mind, the precise execution of those plans determines the usefulness of the end result. Many builders end up frustrating the architect by not following the design. In the case of marriage, the end result of not following God's design is creating something other than what He intended. That's a blueprint for disaster.

A couple of years ago, our church moved from a university basketball gymnasium into a newly purchased warehouse facility. Of course, a big, wide-open warehouse provides a lot of space for a large church, but without some substantial changes, the building isn't suitable for Sunday morning gatherings. For one thing, the acoustics and appearance were not conducive for meetings. But like most churches, budget was an issue, and we were determined to save some money. We put together four teams of volunteers to construct the interior walls of our new auditorium. The architect had designed a complex façade for the four walls which would enclose our meeting area. An elaborate set of blueprints showed us how to attach many glue-lam beams and an array of various building materials into different but beautiful patterns. The team that I was assigned to was tasked with building the front stage area, which included sound pillars on each side of the stage and decorative prism designs holding two large-screen monitors, one on each side of the stage.

In the center of the room, we had built some large tables that became the command post of our crew. There at the command post, we had some guys who were really good at reading blueprints and able to show us where to attach each beam and each bracket and each corbel, so what we built actually took on the look the architect was shooting for when he designed it. At one point, as we neared completion, our senior pastor and other members of the team inspected our work and exclaimed, "Yes, we will be able to use this for gatherings on Sundays, just as the architect intended."

Of course, a bunch of guys running around with nail guns and a pile of lumber could have built a stage and walls without a set of blueprints, but there is no guarantee what it would look like when completed. We could have put the stage in the corner and decided that the large screen monitors look better on the other side of the room. Who knows? We could have decided the pillars that housed the speakers were not even necessary, and when we looked at the final project, it might even seem pleasing to the eye, but would not be very usable during a Sunday morning meeting of about one thousand people. The pastor and the other members of the team may have looked at our design and said, "Thanks for building this, but since you didn't follow the blueprint, we won't be able use it on Sunday."

Now according to the Bible, there are several reasons why the build-as-you-go model just doesn't work, because it creates something unintended, like a poorly planned auditorium. In the same manner, marriages always seem to fall into difficulties and trouble. Why?

First Reason: Conspiracy Theory

According to the Bible, there is an evil conspiracy that is working against all marriages. Marriage is God's idea and God's plan, and Satan doesn't want it to succeed at all. Even for those that don't believe in or follow God's plans. This theory states that there are some sinister forces preventing you from succeeding. Think about that. Are you equipped to handle marriage on your own if this is true?

> *Old-book knowledge*: Be sober-minded; be watchful. Your adversary the devil prowls around like a roaring lion, seeking someone to devour. (1 Pet. 5:8, ESV)

Second Reason: Breaking Bad

The second reason our marriages seem to fall into difficulties and trouble is we basically don't do what is good. There are ideas out there that say man is basically good and will do the right things when given the opportunity, but the Bible says that man is basically bad and in need of help. Usually, when a person finds himself in a bad way in his marriage, it isn't simply because he made a bad decision; it is because he didn't do good, and he didn't treat his spouse right, he didn't say the right thing, he didn't care, and he wasn't very loving. Build-as-you-go gives way too much opportunity for doing the wrong thing.

> *Old-book knowledge*: All have turned aside; together they have become worthless; no one does good, not even one. (Rom. 3:12, ESV)

Third Reason: Liar, Liar

Once you realize that your loved one has lied to you, you can hear that giant sucking sound of love leaving your marriage. We are basically not attracted to people who lie to us; in fact, we tend to dislike and even disdain those who lie to us. Lies and deceptions are a natural product of the build-as-you-go marriage. Without a plan, we often default to "fake it until you make it." Love ends where lies begin and vice-a-versa.

> *Old-book knowledge*: Their throat is an open grave; they use their tongues to deceive. The venom of asps is under their lips. (Rom. 3:13, ESV)

Fourth Reason: Revenge

Revenge is the language of selfishness and is never kind in its responses. We justify bad behavior as righteous revenge on our spouse. It never ceases to amaze me how couples who are arguing get caught up in calling each other names, even using four-letter words. Most people are more reserved in the counseling room than they are in the privacy of their home, but some are more than willing to share with you the language abuses used against them by their partner when no one else was around. For some reason, most of us understand that improper language use is abusive behavior, and we control ourselves when we are in the public's eye, but the rules seem to change within our own four walls. I will usually tell a husband or wife who are feeling fully justified in their outburst, "If you can't speak to the clerk at Wal-Mart that way without the clerk calling security, your behavior is abusive." The language of revenge is always inappropriate and never leads to a satisfactory outcome.

> *Old-book knowledge*: Their mouth is full of curses and bitterness. (Rom. 3:14, ESV).

Fifth Reason: No Fear

Our culture applauds the fearless, but fear has its place in good decisions. The fear of making mistakes is a good, healthy fear. If you have a careless approach to your marriage, you probably don't have a healthy fear of failure and the consequences of failure. Couples with kids generally have a healthier fear of failure in their marriage because they realize that the consequences for the children they love are dangerous. The Bible encourages us in its blueprint to have the fear of God as part of our motivation for getting it right and doing the right things when it comes to our marriage.

> *Old-book knowledge*: There is no fear of God before their eyes. (Rom. 3:18, ESV)

Go with a Blueprint

- Get help with the conspiracy (church, pastor, Christian counselor)
- Identify and stop bad behavior
- Quit practicing lies and deception
- Be kind, not revengeful
- Have a healthy fear of failure

Counselor Notes

Let me tell you about a couple who I counseled with not too long ago, Barry and Cindy. Barry, a career military man, would be considered by most to be quite the catch: handsome, intelligent, hardworking, and very respectful. He does not consider himself an atheist or agnostic, but he doesn't really have any beliefs when it comes to God. He just wants to live his life the best he can and not bother anyone. Cindy, who was an administrative assistant with a very pleasant personality and a certain attractive naiveté, placed an ad on a dating website and hooked up with Barry. Cindy was raised in a home with Christian values, but she never really practiced her faith until meeting up with a Campus Crusade group in college. These two fell in love and got engaged, and then ended up in my office asking for advice.

After finding all about their situation, I explained to Cindy that it is not God's will for her to marry someone who is not a believer and who is not striving to live for Christ. Cindy had felt an internal struggle brewing, and that is why she brought Barry with her to my office. I was just confirming what she already knew to be true, but she was just hoping that I would somehow give her a glimmer of hope to marry Barry, or at least to convince him that he needed Jesus. Barry thought the whole thing was ridiculous because, on the one hand, everybody was telling him that he has the free will to choose God or not, but on the other hand, I was telling Cindy she was not free to marry him if he did not choose God. "How is that free will?" he questioned me point blank.

I explained to Barry that it would not be the best situation for him to marry Cindy because, ultimately, her desire for a biblical marriage would lead to disappointment that he wouldn't appreciate in a spouse. It would lead to conflict between them. Barry said, "It doesn't matter as long as we love each other and are happy together. I believe in God. I don't have to believe in all of that other stuff the same as Cindy."

I told Barry that he only had three choices for his beliefs: One: Believe that there is no God, and everything is totally random, accidental, and ultimately meaningless. For this choice, he is right that any marriage arrangement will do. Two: Believe that there is a God, but He hasn't revealed himself to us, and therefore, we don't know what He wants, so once again, any marriage arrangement or belief system will do. Three: Believe that there is a God, who has revealed Himself to us, and we better find out what beliefs and actions are necessary as well as what marriage arrangements are acceptable to Him. If God has revealed Himself to humans, then we will have some blueprints from His creation to follow.

Marriage Is God's Creation

Creation matters! Many people, like Barry, believe in God, but at the same time, have a passive belief in what their school textbooks taught them as well. Many have been taught that life evolved, and even if God is knowable, He is not necessary or preferred when it comes to explaining origins. A knowable God coexisting with a theory of origins independent of God is the most illogical belief system that a person can have. God and the various theories of evolution are incompatible and mutually exclusive. If evolution and God could coexist, God is nothing more than an unrevealed and unknowable force just like evolution, and He is content to let life and the systems around life, like marriage, change and develop over time without purpose.

In the case of evolution, marriage as a system would not need to exist, but since it does, it must at least change and develop into new forms over long periods of time, just like biological life. But the God of the Bible is a God who has revealed Himself as a God of purpose and order. Genesis 1:1, 31 (ESV) says, "In the beginning God created the Heavens and the Earth...God saw all that he had made, and it was very good. God created man in His image to be in relationship with Him, and He created systems for mankind to live in relationship with each other, like a blueprint of how to live in harmony and love. If evolution is true, there is no need for marriage or a blueprint. Marriage, when present, would be like man, ever-changing, and relational systems like cohabitation, step families, gay marriage, and plural marriage are just expected random developments in an unguided system.

If macro-evolution is the predominant force, or what we can call creation without a blueprint, and if it is a viable option for the explanation of life systems, then it is hard to explain why marriage has always been around and even exists.

If man is slowly evolving through struggle and reproduction, relationships that slow down, monitor reproduction, and limit selection are oddly against natural law. After all, most animals have no such system. If evolution is true, there is no design or blueprint for people, and marriage is random and irrelevant. It doesn't matter how a person reproduces if the purpose isn't clearly defined. But in God's grand design for marriage, union in marriage has purpose, and is itself a form of creation. Genesis 2:24 (ESV) describes marriage: "When a man leaves his father and mother and is united to his wife they become one flesh. Two becoming one is the creation of a new single unit."

As individuals, we also become a new creation when we receive Christ and become one with Him. Galatians 3:28 (ESV) explains: For you are all one in Christ Jesus. Just as the world was made by God, we who receive Him by believing in His name are born of God. The apostle John explains: "Yet to all who did receive him, to those who believed in his name, he gave the right to become children of

God." (Jn 1:12, ESV). This regeneration of our soul is a new work of creation performed by Christ Jesus. We cannot fully receive Christ if we do not accept the full implication of His name. To receive Christ is to understand that He is God. He is the Creator of all things, the Word made flesh to dwell among us. To receive and believe Jesus as anything other than the Creator is to not receive Him at all. He must be our Creator before He can be our Savior and Redeemer and call us His own. If He is not the Creator, He could not give us an inheritance as His sons or children, and there would be no power of adoption where He adopts us into His family, and no power or purpose even in marriage since He is the one who joins two in marriage. This is what Mark 10:9 (ESV) tells us, therefore what God has joined together, let no one separate. But because God did create the heavens and the earth, marriage, like man, does have purpose as well as divine design, and God provides a blueprint that can and should be followed to fulfill His desires for our marital purpose. Barry and Cindy could go ahead and get married, but they would not be following God's creative design for a husband and wife. God commands us: "Do not be yoked together with unbelievers. For what do righteousness and wickedness have in common? Or what fellowship can light have with darkness?" (2 Cor. 6:14, ESV). This tells us that we cannot achieve God's purposes in marriage unless we follow His rules.

Conspiracy Theory

The apostle Paul addresses this question fairly well in Romans 3. In verse 10, he says, "There is no one that seeks God." If we are really truthful about this, we have to admit that we aren't really seeking out God's purpose for our marriage—or anything else in our life for that matter. We tend to do things our way, and then we reach out for God when it goes bad. The apostle tells us this is our overall human condition. None of us seek out God or His design for marriage, and without God, we don't have a workable drawing. God's design is perfect; if we follow it, then marriage works. If we fail to follow it, then we get what we get, and rarely are we satisfied with the results.

Breaking Bad

According to Romans 3:12, there is no one who does good. When two sinners get married, bad things can happen. Rarely when my wife, Fran, gets upset with me, am I totally innocent and undeserving of her reaction. Of course, two wrongs never add up to a right, and so we end up running off the track, caught up in some conflict. But why are we always so surprised when bad things happen because of our bad behavior? Probably because even though we know we don't do good, we don't really see ourselves as bad, as sinners. This is more proof that we really aren't seeking God.

Liar, Liar

We are basically not attracted to people who lie to us; in fact, we tend to dislike and even disdain those who lie to us. Satan is the father of lies. He lies to us because he doesn't regard us as valuable and doesn't care what happens to us. God always tells us the truth because He does care for us and He does value us. He will even tell us the hard truths because He doesn't want us walking off a cliff or into a pit. Satan could care less; he would just laugh at you as you were falling.

The greatest danger of not being truthful is when we are not truthful with ourselves. When it comes to talking to yourself, you are the best salesman you know. If I set my mind to it, I could wake up in the morning and convince myself that I need to buy a new truck, and by the end of the day, drive that new truck into my driveway. This could be the case even if I didn't need a new truck. I can talk myself into or out of just about anything. We all have the ability to sell ourselves on just about anything. You can tell yourself that your marriage is bad and unbearable and that you don't have a choice but to divorce. You can look at something that your spouse has done and convince yourself that she (or he) doesn't really love you because of it. Of course, none of this has to be even remotely true, but you can convince yourself of it.

Revenge

The fourth reason our marriages fall into difficulty and trouble is that we are selfish and unkind. According to the apostle Paul, our mouth is full of cursing and bitterness (Romans 3:14). Most of the spouses would not even dream of speaking to me abusively in my office because they understand that I would probably bounce them out on their ear, but for some reason, it doesn't click that they are abusers when they practice this at home with each other. Many men are even devastated at the thought of being called an abuser; they even take pride in not being physically aggressive with their wives, and yet they openly admit to speaking to their wives in inappropriate ways.

No Fear

Finally, our marriages tend to fall into difficulty and trouble because we don't really fear God. Romans 3:18 says, we have no fear of God at all. If we really feared God, it would definitely change the way that we treat each other in marriage. If we really believed we will stand before God someday and answer for every idle word spoken, it would change the way we live our life, especially in marriage. If we really feared God, knowing that someday we will answer for the way we treat our wife or our husband, our marriage would look a whole lot different than it currently does. We don't call God an outright liar and say that we don't believe Him. However, our actions prove our lack of fear when dealing with God, because if we really feared Him, it would affect the way that we live.

Our behavior really says a lot about what we truly believe. For example, if you were sitting at the dinner table one evening, having dinner with your wife, and I called you up and said, "This is Gary; I have it on good authority that a tornado is heading straight for your house!"

You hang up the phone, look at your wife, and say, "Please pass the potatoes."

And she responds, "Who was that on the phone?"

You say, "Oh that was Gary."

She responds, "What did he want?"

You say, "Something about a tornado heading straight toward our house."

She says, "Oh really."

Without taking a breath, you say, "What are we going to do after dinner?"

In this scenario, you didn't jump up and down and call me a liar and argue with me about what I said. You just didn't really believe that the tornado was heading toward your home. If you really believed that the tornado was heading straight for your house, it would have affected the way you responded. You would have jumped up from the dinner table and started gathering your things and getting your wife and kids out of the house and into the car and out of the neighborhood.

It's true. Our behavior says a lot about what we truly believe. Marriage is a spiritual battleground, and as such, tests our resolve. If we believe that God is the creator and designer of marriage and that our marriage is very important to Him, then that belief will flush itself out in our daily lives. The tornado is coming, and when we just live our lives as if there is no problem, that tells us a little something about our faith. Marriage is actually a barometer measuring God's influence on your life. Creation matters, and God has designed marriage for divine use within His creation, and this should affect the way that we live and practice marriage.

Questions for Group Discussion

- Have you been following the build-as-you-go plan for your marriage? How is that working?
- What is the biggest objection you have to using the old book knowledge in the Bible for your marriage?
- Do you believe the conspiracy theory? Why or why not?
- Are people generally good or bad? How can you test your view?

- Why do lies hurt marriage so much?
- How does revenge play a role in marriage?
- What is healthy fear? Explain your view of fear's place in marriage.

2

Starting Point: The Foundation

Very few buildings are built without a foundation, and without a foundation, a building is temporary at best. The structure of the foundation seems to determine the longevity of the building itself. I have seen buildings outlast their foundations, but they are moved to a new foundation to continue on. A few years ago, a historic Victorian home was plucked from its old foundation in our neighborhood and moved to a new location nearby. The crew scheduled to move the old house at two or three in the morning, and a few of us venturesome souls lined the streets in our city to watch this feat of technology as this old Victorian home was moved several miles across town. Of course, many days of preparation to the lot that would receive this old home had already taken place. The new foundation had to be in place and the home, once raised over the foundation, had to be meticulously lowered and attached to that foundation. This assured continuous support from that foundation and longevity for the home itself.

The same can be said for our marriage. We must meticulously attach our marriage to a foundation for support if we are to have longevity and stability. Old-book knowledge tells us that foundations are important for longevity, especially when it comes to marriage and family.

> *Old-book knowledge*: Everyone then who hears these words of mine and does them will be like a wise man who built his house on the rock. And the rain fell, and the floods came, and the winds blew and beat on that house, but it did not fall, because it had been founded on the rock. (Matt. 7:23–25, ESV)

How do we build our marriage on a rock? There are five basic steps to a solid foundation. They are mapped out on the blueprint, helping us to complete our site preparation and giving us a solid foundation for our build. These basic steps also give us five important principles of marriage.

1. Compaction: Commitment

If the soil beneath the foundation is not firm, the foundation will crack and crumble. Compaction assures that no unwanted movement will take place. This is what we call an all-in commitment; unmovable, unshakeable, dependable, and firm.

An all-in commitment means you are willing to give up your life for the other person if necessary. If you're just beginning in marriage, you'll need to begin with compaction. If your marriage has already moved and cracked and your foundation is faulty, you'll need to start over and create a new foundation. Begin with an all-in commitment. This is the first principle of marriage.

Old-book knowledge: Be faithful unto death, and I will give you the crown of life. (Rev. 2:10, ESV)

2. Forming: Sexual Fidelity

What would happen to your relationship right now if your spouse or fiancé or even your boyfriend or girlfriend were to be found messing around with someone else? Whatever the specific outcome, it wouldn't be good, would it? Therefore, sexual fidelity becomes a basic and important principle for marriage. Sexual fidelity sets good healthy boundaries that help us function better in relationships both before and during marriage. Sexual fidelity is the second basic principle for marriage. It is a no-brainer. It is the reason we get married in the first place, to have an exclusive relationship in a meaningful way. Sexual fidelity forms the boundaries for this exclusive relationship.

Old-book knowledge: I wrote to you in my letter not to associate with sexually immoral people. (1 Cor. 5:9, ESV)

3. Rock: Substance

Rock is what separates concrete from mortar. Mortar can have the appearance of concrete, but if you try to put a building on a foundation of mortar, it's going to crumble and fall. Looking at the overall blueprint for a building, the foundation specifications are detailed, the greater the building, the greater the foundation. What is the substance of your relationship? Is it rock or is it sand? I'm sure you've already heard that relationships built on physical attraction are like buildings being built on sand, they're not going to last through any kind of storm or something similar. Does your marriage have a foundation that can be built or re-built on? This is the third basic principle for marriage.

Old-book knowledge: Built on the foundation of the apostles and prophets, Christ Jesus himself being the cornerstone. (Eph. 2:20, ESV)

4. Rebar: Strength

Most concrete foundations are meshed with rebar to build strength into the slab or footings. Rebar is used as the primary reinforcement of concrete for carrying heavy tension loads, and it is also used as a secondary reinforcement to help with aesthetics, limiting stress fractures, and cracking. Does your marriage have some primary and secondary reinforcement? Does positive reinforcement from social entities shore you up? How about supportive family and friends? Whatever it is, you need it because even spectacular marriages, like spectacular buildings, need reinforced foundations. This is the fourth basic principle of marriage.

Old-book knowledge: But the Helper, the Holy Spirit, whom the Father will send in my name, he will teach you all things. (Jn 14:26, ESV)

5. Cement: Contentment

The day after we get married, we realize that our partner is imperfect in some way, and we begin to convince ourselves that we cannot live with our partner until the imperfections are corrected. We might say, "I wish my wife was more like his wife." Or, "I wish my husband did things more like her husband." But we do better to be content with the husband or wife that we already have. There seems to be more than just anecdotal evidence these days that positive emotions contribute to psychological and physical well-being. We need to dwell on those positive things that our spouse brings to the relationship and not on the negative traits or other areas in which our spouse is deficient. We sometimes get caught up in "the grass is greener on the other side of the fence" syndrome. Well, the grass is greener on the other side of the fence because they actually water it over there, because their septic tank is broken and fertilizer is flowing everywhere. Either way, contentment becomes a very important fifth principle to uphold in our marriage.

Old-book Knowledge: But godliness with contentment is great gain. (1 Tim. 6:6, ESV)

These five principles are not easy to apply to a marriage. Many times, our habits can trip us up, or the world around us will tell us that we don't need to work so hard on getting our attitudes right. We have a whole commercial industry teaching us to be discontent with what we have, and sometimes, when we are in a bad marriage, it becomes overwhelming. Our first thought is to bail and start over instead of getting back to basics by following the directions. The problem with bailing out and starting over is that we still end up with an inferior product if we don't follow the designer's directions.

Go with a Blueprint

- Begin with an all-in commitment or start again with an all-in commitment
- Be sexually faithful
- Base your relationship on substance
- Help your marriage with reinforcement
- Be content with your partner

Counselor Notes

If we are to have longevity and stability in our marriage, we must meticulously attach our marriage to a foundation for support. Where can we find this foundation for our marriage? We must find our support in Jesus Christ, more specifically, in His Word. Jesus tells us that not listening to His Word is like building a house without establishing a decent foundation. He says, "And everyone who hears these words of mine and does not do them will be like a foolish man who built his house on the sand. And the rain fell, and the floods came, and the winds blew and beat against that house, and it fell, and great was the fall of it." (Matt. 7:26–27, ESV).

Yes, we must look to the words of Christ for foundation, but sometimes, as we try to strengthen marriages in our churches, we direct ourselves specifically to the marriage passages in the Bible and avoid other Scriptures. All of God's Word speaks to our marriage relationship, not just a select few passages. The specific passages about marriage are found in 1 Corinthians 7, 1 Peter 3, Ephesians 5, or Colossians 3. But we also need to consider the entire body of Scripture when it comes to learning about marriage. Any time we read about how to have proper behavior and proper attitudes and generally how to act or think as revealed to us within the pages of God's Word, we need to apply those commands and principles to our marriage. From now on, I would like you to consider everything you hear from God's Word and tell yourself, "Oh yeah, this applies to my marriage as well."

When your pastor is preaching about something that does not especially pertain to marriage, remember that you may need to apply the principle to the relationship with your wife or the relationship with your husband.

If you find yourself approaching a passage, and you have some uncertainty as far as its application to your marriage, you can do what I do: Apply the "exception test." Let me demonstrate. The apostle Paul tells us: "Let all bitterness and wrath and anger and clamor and slander be put away from you, along with all malice. Be kind to one another, tenderhearted, forgiving one another, as God in Christ forgave you." (Eph. 4:31–32, ESV). Now, if you want to see if this passage should apply to your marriage, insert the exception: Get rid of all bitterness, rage, and anger, brawling and slander, along with every form of malice, "except when dealing with my husband" when he doesn't behave right and be kind and compassionate to one another, forgiving each other, just as in Christ God forgave you, "except when my wife is being unreasonable toward me." Do those exceptions make any sense? Of course not, God's standard for your marriage relationship is not less than His standard for your other relationships—if anything, it is more.

Foundational Principles from Ephesians

Ephesians 5 is a great place to demonstrate this truth. In the first half of Ephesians 5, the apostle Paul is speaking to the entire church at Ephesus. In the second half of Ephesians 5, he begins to speak directly to husbands and wives. We have much to learn when he speaks directly to husbands and wives, but it is interesting that as he speaks to the entire church in the first part of the chapter, we can actually pull out of his writings some foundational principles that we should apply to marriage. In verse 1, he begins by explaining that we should be imitators of God; we now have a starting point, the beginnings of a model or blueprint to follow. I enjoy telling this story of a young newlywed couple, because when a couple first gets married, people like to ask them the question, "How is it going?" People are curious about how the new relationship is progressing. The wife of this one particular couple had her own way of dealing with this question. Any time somebody would ask her, "How is it going?" she would say, "Great, my husband is the model husband." If her relatives asked her, "How is it going?" she would say, "Great, my husband is the model husband." If they were out with friends, and they asked, "How is it going?" she would say, "Great, my husband is the model husband." Her husband began to feel pretty good about himself and his marriage, until one day, he was sitting around the house, killing time, and he decided to grab a dictionary off the shelf and look up the word *model*. The definition read, "Model: A cheap imitation of the real thing." Now he wasn't so sure that his wife had been complimenting him.

In reality, we will never live up to God's example, and when we imitate God, we are always going to be a cheap imitation of the real thing, but He does give us an example. He does give us a blueprint to help us build according to His design.

Principle 1: Commitment

Using the guideline of imitating God and applying all of God's Word to our marriage, we can glean at least five basic principles for marriage. In Ephesians 5:2 (ESV), we read: "And walk in love, as Christ loved us and gave himself up for us, a fragrant offering and sacrifice to God." To walk in love the way that Christ walked in love with us and gave Himself up for us requires us to have commitment. Christ gave His life for us. This means He was fully committed to us, He was all in, and there is no greater commitment than to give up your life for someone or something. This becomes the first principle of marriage: "all-in commitment." Without commitment, you don't have a marriage. Commitment is the starting point and not something that we are working toward.

But commitment doesn't always come first with a couple. Many couples today begin their relationship with sex, not a commitment. Pastor Tommy Nelson, founder of the Song of Solomon marriage conferences, says that sex before marriage is like a paper fire. I don't know about you, but I love a good paper fire. Paper fires burn big and fast and are fun to watch, but ultimately, they do not last and are not all that useful. When building a fire, what we really need are logs or coal because they burn bright and hot and have longevity. When we begin a relationship with sex, we're working backward. We create an unnatural connection and a mysterious bond that affects our judgment. Relationships that begin with sex are highly likely to fail, but relationships that begin with commitment are highly likely to succeed.

In our culture today, we've created a new system for love and marriage. Couples hook up, have sex, and decide to live together. The reasoning is usually to try out the relationship before making a commitment and thus avoid making the mistake of marrying the wrong person. In this scenario, the lie that many have bought into is, a person can have sex with someone and then walk away—no harm, no foul if the relationship doesn't work out. Sex has been part of God's design for the marriage relationship since the beginning; it symbolizes the mysterious joining together of the husband and wife as one. It is not just symbolic, but the physical act itself mysteriously bonds the two of them together. The Bible describes this: "Therefore a man shall leave his father and his mother and hold fast to his wife, and they shall become one flesh." (Gen. 2:24, ESV).

When you glue two pieces of paper together, the two pieces become bonded as one, and though they remain two separate pieces of paper, they are functioning as one. Once bonded, they are not meant to be separated, and separating can actually cause damage. Both pieces may end up torn and tattered with pieces of the one permanently stuck to the other in spots. It is for this reason that many couples who have tried living together and then discovered that they are with the wrong person try to correct that error by getting married. They started with the paper fire and then worked toward commitment and then decided, "Uh oh, wrong person." But now, bonded through sex, feel compelled to try marriage in order to correct their mistake. No wonder the rate of divorce for couples who cohabitate before marriage is disturbingly high.[1]

Living together before making the marriage commitment is not the solution, and even those couples who are successful in making the split and moving on are not experiencing "no harm, no foul," but just the opposite. They seem to experience all the same emotional turmoil of couples who divorce after making the marriage commitment after living together. God doesn't tell us that sex should only be part of a committed marriage relationship to spoil our fun, but He knows something about us that we don't.

What Does God Know That We Don't?

Sex is not just something that people do for fun; it is not something that should be practiced outside of relationship, but it is an act that mysteriously bonds us to another even without the marriage commitment. We begin to understand this concept by reading 1 Corinthians 6:16 (ESV): "Or do you not know that he who is joined to a prostitute becomes one body with her? For, as it is written, 'the two will become one flesh.'" You see, God knows more about you than you know about yourself. Verse 18 goes on to say: "Flee from sexual immorality. Every other sin a person commits is outside the body, but the sexually immoral person sins against his own body."

God is the Creator, and He is our Creator. He knows every intricate detail about us, and we don't really know squat about ourselves. When you go to bed tonight, you will be breathing all night long. Why don't you decide not to do that? Why don't you decide before going to bed tonight that you're going to take a break and not breathe all night long? Your brain sends signals to your heart all day long to make sure that it keeps beating. Why don't you decide to give that procedure a rest? Your cells are multiplying and dividing continuously in a process that keeps you living. Why don't you decide to interfere with that process? You see, you don't really know jack squat about yourself, but God, your Creator, does. He knows how, why, and in what situations you will work best. When it comes to marriage, commitment before sex is how we will function best, and how we can build something by God's design, by honoring Him, and thereby benefitting us.

So God's design and blueprint for marriage is a strong argument for "paperclip dating." If sex bonds us like glue to another person, then we certainly don't want to be bonded before we are sure we want to make that lifelong commitment. When two pieces of paper are just paper clipped together, it might leave a little indentation when separated, but a paperclip indentation can be smoothed out without leaving permanent damage. In a paperclip relationship, we can work toward a lifelong commitment, and at one point, if we decide, "Uh oh, wrong person," then we can walk away with no harm or no foul.

On the other hand, relationships that stop short of sexual intercourse before marriage, but still go too far physically before a commitment, could be like being stapled together. They won't be as severely damaged as when separated after glue bonding, but they will still have noticeable signs of damage that cannot be repaired.

Not long ago, I met with a young newlywed couple, Bruce and Lisa. Bruce was a very personable, mild-mannered young man working toward becoming a missionary for his church. Lisa was a very supportive wife, though somewhat fragile in nature. Bruce had spent his years in college involved in various dating experiences, and though he was convinced that he needed to avoid actual intercourse, he wasn't as convinced to avoid having very physically oriented relationships in other ways. After just a few weeks of marriage, he began having difficulty in physical relations with his wife. He couldn't maintain enough excitement to finish with her without thinking about other women, reminding him of various physical stimulations he had associated with relationships in the past.

Bruce may not have been torn and ripped from the bonding created by intercourse and physical union with another woman before commitment, but he was damaged, affecting not only himself, but his new wife. Inappropriate dating had left a mark on his life, much like a staple in a piece of paper. This is not an insurmountable obstacle in their marriage, but with Lisa's extra sensitivity about all things relational, it will not be a problem easily ignored either. God's design protects us from this unnecessary damage, and God's blueprint for marriage begins with commitment before sex.

Principle 2: Sexual Purity

The second principle of marriage we find cradled in Ephesians 5:3–5 is sexual purity. Without sexual purity, a couple doesn't have a marriage. Verse 5 tells us that the sexually immoral person will not inherit the kingdom of God, and whenever the Bible gives us a list of sins that will bring God's punishment or wrath upon man, sexual impurity or immorality is always mentioned among that list. God's standard for His church is that these kinds of sin should not even be named among us.

The topic of sexual purity goes right to our relationship with God. Show me someone who can maintain sexual purity, and I'll show you someone who can maintain a healthy relationship with God, but show me someone who struggles with sexual purity, and I'll show you someone who struggles in his relationship with God. Man's relationship with God seems to have always had a sexual element to it. In Genesis 3, Adam and Eve, after they had sinned, realized for the first time that they were naked. It seems somewhat odd that they would not have understood their nakedness before that moment, but it is likely that the mysterious light that comes from God (who is light), the light that existed before the sun the moon and the stars were created, was the same glorious light that God used to "clothe" Adam and Eve. Moses may have also exhibited this same light coming down from the high place with God, clothed in His Shekinah glory. Perfection, purity, and sinlessness are things that we cannot completely relate to in this marred, cursed, and fallen world that we currently live in. But Adam and Eve, when they first lived in the garden, knew a more perfect world.

First Timothy 2:14 says, "And Adam was not deceived, but the woman was deceived and became a transgressor," Adam was not deceived, but he did sin. I used to struggle understanding the point of this verse, but now I believe that I have some understanding. Eve was deceived because Satan is a great liar. Some of the best lies always have a little bit of truth in them. Satan said to Eve, "You won't die if you eat this fruit." And Eve didn't die physically immediately, but she did begin to die, and it could be said that, spiritually, she died immediately and lost that glorious clothing of light that we talked about.

Satan also said to Eve, "If you eat this, you will be like God." It's true that Eve was a little bit like God in her understanding of good and evil for the first time after eating the fruit. For the first time ever, she realized that there was now evil and not all good in the world. She lost her naïveté, but she was nothing like God. The connotation is that Eve was deceived, but Adam was not; Adam just chose Eve

24

over God. Eve had chosen the taste and beauty of the fruit and the promise of earthly wisdom over her relationship with God, and Adam had chosen the form and beauty of the woman and the promise of earthly companionship over his relationship with God. Adam chose his sexuality over his relationship with God. This makes perfect sense because that is what men have been doing ever since. God created Eve and sexual pleasure for Adam, but He still wanted to know that Adam loved Him more than what He had created (Eve) for Adam. Sexual purity helps us relate with God in a pure way.

Principle 3: Know God's Will

A third principle of marriage in Ephesians 5 is to know God's will. We are to know God's will and then to live in it. I am devoting a whole chapter to knowing God's will, so I will not elaborate here, but it goes back to the opening discussion of how we are not seeking God, and, therefore, not seeking His will. This causes our relationships to fall into difficulty and trouble. Understanding God's will requires a personal transformation and subjection of our own bodies, presenting them as living sacrifices to God. A marriage conformed to God's will is not only good and acceptable, but it is perfected in the Lord Jesus Christ, perfected by His blueprint. This perfection allows us to also perfect our relationship with our spouse.

Principle 4: Be Filled with the Holy Spirit

The fourth principle of marriage is to be filled with His Spirit. "And do not get drunk with wine, for that is debauchery, but be filled with the Spirit." (Eph. 5:18, ESV). Notice that we are commanded to be filled with the Spirit. We are given a prescription here to take, and there is an act of will involved.

We can choose to allow God's Spirit to fill us, or we can choose to quench God's Spirit working in our life by living outside God's will. I will boldly proclaim here that two Spirit-filled individuals will not struggle in their marriage. When a couple comes into my office for crisis counseling, they are not two Spirit-filled individuals seeking God and growing in His will. Usually, one or both of them have shot off the reservation and are in disobedience to God's will and ignoring His Spirit's leading in their life. If the fruits of the Spirit are not evident in your marriage but appear evident in other areas of your life, it is probably all pretense. The fruit of the Spirit produces love in your marriage, that is: patient and not easily angered; kind, not rude; truthful without evil intent; persevering, not selfish or prideful; protective, not resentful or envious, and, hopefully, trusting without being arrogant. "But the fruit of the Spirit is love, joy, peace, patience, kindness, goodness, faithfulness, gentleness, self-control; against such things there is no law." (Gal. 5:22–23, ESV). The true gauge of a Spirit-filled life is the relationship you have with your husband or wife. It is here where God will prepare you for work elsewhere that He has prepared for you, and it is here where you can be disqualified as well. And it is here that you can develop a wonderful relationship with your wife or husband. It is impossible for marriage to fail when both individuals are being led and influenced by the Holy Spirit in their lives.

Principle 5: Contentment

The fifth principle discovered in these pages written to the entire church at Ephesus is contentment. In verse 20, we are told to give thanks always for all things to God the Father in the name of the Lord Jesus Christ. In always giving thanks, we are showing an outward sign of an inward contentment. The apostle Paul writes, "Godliness with contentment is great gain." (1 Tim. 6:6, ESV). God wants you to be content in your marriage, but usually, we plant our own seeds of discontentment.

These five principles are necessary for marriage, but we often stray from our relationship with God. Our building begins to crumble—even with our best intentions. Disaster is just a little ways in the distance. That's why we need to work on the framework we build for our building. What we build on our foundation will make the difference. The foundation secures what we build, but the framework protects us in so many ways. We will learn about this framework in the next chapter.

Questions for Group Discussion

- Have you made and all-in commitment? What barriers do you have for starting over with this kind of commitment?
- Have you been sexually faithful? Are you willing to be?
- How has infidelity affected your life?
- What are some things of substance you can build your marriage on? (Society, family, children, God?)
- Where will you find reinforcement for your marriage?
- Are you a content person? What advantages does having positive attitudes give to marriage?
- Will you make any changes to build a firm foundation with which to build? Why or why not?

3

The Framework

The framework of the building is nothing without a good foundation, but it is the most important part of a building that we identify and use. A good framework determines what a house or building will look like from the outside. It determines its style, whether modern or Victorian or craftsman, etc. It determines its functionality: whether a house, an office building, a warehouse, or a church. Framework determines suitable functionality and, in many cases, limits functionality. At our church, we have converted warehouses into a church campus. We have unlimited storage capacity compared to most churches, but we are very limited in office space and classrooms. We have a good foundation, so we can change the framework and build something more suitable for our needs as time progresses. The same is true of your marriage. If you have a good foundation, you can change the framework. If you've built something unsuitable, rebuild and build something beautiful that is useful.

> *Old-book knowledge*: And if you will listen to all that I command you, and will walk in my ways, and do what is right in my eyes by keeping my statutes and my commandments, as David my servant did, I will be with you and will build you a sure house. (1 Kgs 11:38, ESV)

Framework: Authority

Submit to the authorities in your life. Good organization always needs leaders in authority to prevent chaos. It sounds good to do what you want to do, go where you want to go, and be what you want to be, but when everybody is running around, doing only what they want to do without submitting to authority, we have chaos, and it's only fun to be free when everything else around you is organized. Give up a little freedom and submit to authority, and you will enjoy the freedoms you have much more. Organize your marriage and quit being so independent, and you will actually be freer to enjoy each other.

> *Old-book knowledge*: Look carefully then how you walk, not as unwise but as wise, making the best use of the time, because the days are evil. Therefore do not be foolish, but understand what the will of the Lord is. And do not get drunk with wine, for that is debauchery, but be filled with the Spirit, addressing one another in psalms and hymns and spiritual songs, singing and making melody to the Lord with your heart, giving thanks always and for everything to God the Father in the name of our Lord Jesus Christ, submitting to one another out of reverence for Christ. (Eph. 5:15–21, ESV)

Framework: Husband as Leader

I know, not politically correct. Remember, we are following someone else's blueprint. We could design it ourselves, but we may not be happy with the result. No one in charge sounds good, but will end up with everyone being unhappy and arguing. Remember, the goal is organization, not dictatorship. The wife as the leader could work, but that isn't the design. If you don't follow the blueprint, you're building something, but it may be of no use to the designer when all is said and done.

> *Old-book knowledge*: Wives, submit to your own husbands, as to the Lord. For the husband is the head of the wife even as Christ is the head of the church, his body, and is himself its Savior. Now as the church

submits to Christ, so also wives should submit in everything to their husbands. (Eph. 5:22–24, ESV)

Framework: Wives Protected

Every leader is a cog in an organization and is expected to protect not only the organization, but the values and goals of the organization. The husband, as the leader of the marriage and family, needs to build a framework that fits appropriately on the foundation and promotes the ultimate goals of the designer. One important goal is the care and protection of the wife. The husband cannot be an effective leader within this design without being focused on this goal and using all at his disposal to achieve this objective.

> *Old-book knowledge*: Husbands, love your wives, as Christ loved the church and gave himself up for her, that he might sanctify her, having cleansed her by the washing of water with the word, so that he might present the church to himself in splendor, without spot or wrinkle or any such thing, that she might be holy and without blemish. In the same way husbands should love their wives as their own bodies. He who loves his wife loves himself. For no one ever hated his own flesh, but nourishes and cherishes it, just as Christ does the church, because we are members of his body. (Eph. 5:25–30, ESV)

Framework: Dependence

In many cases, our parents spend a great deal of time and money helping us to be independent. We live in the land of the free and home of the brave, a country built on fierce independence, but this blueprint calls for dependence not independence. Husbands and wives are to be fiercely dependent on one another. Autonomy is an American value, but it is a terrible design for marriage. The more you depend on your spouse, the better your marriage will be. Even leaders aren't independent; their success or failure always hinges on those being led. Followers make or break leaders. If a husband is following his mandate to protect and care for his wife, and the wife is following her husband's leadership, the marriage will flourish. Often, dependence will lead to success where independence will lead to failure. Independence alone did not make the United States a great nation, but the dependence that followed did.

> *Old-book knowledge:* Therefore a man shall leave his father and mother and hold fast to his wife, and the two shall become one flesh. (Eph. 5:31, ESV)

Framework: Mutual Love and Respect

It's hard to go wrong with loving and respecting people. This blueprint calls for both love and respect to be a mutual occurrence in marriage. In general, men have an easier time respecting their wives than loving them, and in general, women do better at loving their husbands than respecting them. Because of these natural tendencies, it is a good plan to concentrate on our weak points. Men should give special attention to loving their wives, and women should give special attention to respecting their husbands.

The end result will be a positive one for your marriage and, according to Emerson Eggerich: "His love motivates her respect and her respect motivates his love."[2]

This sounds like a solid plan for some attractive and useful framework.

> *Old-book knowledge*: However, let each one of you love his wife as himself, and let the wife see that she respects her husband. (Eph. 5:33, ESV)

Get with a Blueprint

- Submit to authorities in your life
- Husbands are the leaders
- Wives are protected

- Be dependent on each other
- Have mutual love and respect

Counselor Notes

Excellent buildings require firm foundations, solid frameworks, and attractive rooflines. When a firm marital foundation is laid—consisting of commitment, sexual purity, knowledge of God's will, Spirit abundance, and contentment—then there is no chance of overwhelming such a foundation with loads too heavy to bear. Jesus Christ represents our foundation and the cornerstone of our entire building process in our life and marriage. We must choose a worthy foundation and dedicate our life to constructing a framework that will hold a crown and give God glory. Our marriage is one aspect of our life that can accomplish this, and marriage must have its own godly framework as well.

Who's the General?

In the second half of Ephesians 5, the apostle Paul lays out the framework for the marriage relationship. First, he tells us to submit to one another in the fear of God. Here, he is still speaking to the whole church, not just to husbands and wives. He uses the Greek word *hupotasso*; this word can have a military connotation to it. In other words, we are to treat others in the church like they are the generals, and we are the privates. Could you imagine how well we would all get along in the church if we treated others like they were the general? Instead, we show up on Sunday and say, "Who moved my table and chairs? Don't they know I need those? Don't they know that what I do is important?" But we could say, "I guess the general needed my tables and chairs, and since I am just a private, I will make do with what I have. The general's needs are more important than mine." This is the attitude that we are commanded to have with one another. Within this context, the apostle Paul shifts gears and begins to speak directly to husbands and wives. Beginning with the wife, he says in verse 22–23, "Submit to your own husbands, as to the Lord. For the husband is the head of the wife even as Christ is the head of the church, his body, and is himself its Savior." Here, he uses the exact same Greek word *hupotasso* for "submit."

In our culture, this is a politically incorrect statement. Our culture says that the wife should not submit to the husband because the wife is equal to the husband, and marriage is a fifty-fifty proposition. But if Paul just told everyone in the church to submit to one another, why would it be such an outrageous statement to command the wife to be submissive to her husband? After all, God's standard in our marriage would not be less than the standard He has for us with others outside of our marriage; if anything, He would require a higher standard within our marriage. Let's try adding an exception to verse 21. "Submit to one another in the fear of God, except for your husband." No, it doesn't work. But the focus does not end with the wife's submission to the husband. The whole blueprint must be read in its entirety for us to understand how all the parts fit together.

Getting Practical

So now the focus shifts toward the husband in verse 25. "Husbands, love your wives, as Christ loved the church and gave himself up for her." How much does Christ love the church? He was all in; He gave His life for the church. So husbands, you are to love your wife and even lay down your life for her if necessary. What this means is that if the situation arises; you should step in and take a bullet for her. Some guys who are kind of macho will say, "Of course, I will take the bullet for her." But will you work two jobs to make sure that she is protected and cared for? Will you put away your X-Box, or will you get rid of your boat or quad runner to make more time for her? God's blueprint requires that you give up your life in how you love her. Occasionally, I will hear a guy say, "I don't have a life anymore; I'm married." My response is, "That's right, and that's the way God intended it to be." Now, I say to the wives, "How hard would it be to submit to your husband's authority if he loves you this way?" You see, both spouses have to work in conjunction for this to be a blueprinted marriage by God's design. If the wife does not submit to her husband as the church submits to

Christ, or the husband does not love his wife as Christ loved the church, you don't have a marriage that follows God's blueprint. It only works if both are fulfilling their role. However, our role and responsibilities do not change even if only the husband or if only the wife is following God's design. God still holds us responsible for our part, even when our spouse is not doing his or her part. Unless both are following God's blueprint, they don't have a marriage designed as God intended. If you don't follow God's plan, you may still experience a personal joy and satisfaction in your relationship with God, but you won't have a blueprint marriage that honors God. It takes both partners doing their part to complete the design. In other words, you can have a great relationship with God as an individual and still have a bad marriage. Godly people are not guaranteed a good marriage by virtue of their individual submission to Christ alone.

God's designed order in marriage is a spiritual command, "That he might sanctify her, having cleansed her by the washing of water with the word, so that he might present the church to himself in splendor, without spot or wrinkle or any such thing, that she might be holy and without blemish." (Eph. 5:26–27, ESV). Husbands sometimes put on the pants in the family for the wrong reason. We say things like, "I am the head of the household, and I want to buy this boat, so we are going to buy this boat." This is not spiritual headship but a misuse of authority. If you are going to make your wife upset, get her upset for the right reasons. For instance, if you stay out late on a Saturday night, and your wife decides that you should not go to church on Sunday morning because you'll both be too tired, don't just roll over and say, "Cool." and start snoring, but provide leadership and say something like, "I'm sorry, sweetheart, but God has not given me permission to sleep in, and I feel that we must be at worship on Sunday morning." Or your wife might express a desire to stop attending the small group Bible study you've been participating in, but you feel God is leading you to continue attending, so you should say, "I feel that God is leading us to participate in this small group, and therefore, we will attend this small group until God directs us differently." This is how you put the pants on in your family. If you're going to upset your wife, upset her for the right reason.

A couple I once met with, Lyle and Christa, were a young but experienced couple in the midst of raising a family, and they were having some marital conflict. So much so, that Christa had become despondent and was ready to throw in the towel. On a scale of 1–10, she rated her marriage a three, but later, she admitted feeling like reconciliation was hopeless. Lyle was a meticulous and well-organized leader of the home, and Christa was a happy-go-lucky, free-spirited, stay-at-home mom with no desire to sweat the details. Lyle would lead his family in every minute detail when it came to everything but spiritual health. The car would have to be parked just so and the household would have to run to his specifications. He was more than willing to make Christa madder than a hornet and cut her no slack to assure that mostly trivial things were done to perfection, but in the areas where he should have been focused: worship, Bible study, prayer, and godly parenting, he allowed Christa more than enough slack to be a free spirit and even negligent. Lyle should have gone out of his way to keep from exasperating his wife in trivial pursuits of perfection and more willing to risk her anger in the godly pursuit of perfection.

The wife's role is to respond to his leadership and trust God to work in his life as the leader. This is why it is so important for women of God to develop a commitment with a godly man before marriage and not just any man they allow themselves to fall in love with. God has made husbands the head of the household to fulfill a spiritual order, and the husband is responsible to see that his wife is washed in the word. Both of these godly roles must be accomplished to make a marriage complete. The husband doesn't have to be an expert in the Word, but he needs to know enough to lead his wife and family in that direction.

Paul writes, "In the same way, husbands should love their wives as their own bodies. He who loves his wife loves himself. For no one ever hated his own flesh, but nourishes and cherishes it, just as Christ does the church." (Eph. 5:28– 29, ESV). This is a verse that gets overlooked, and yet it could transform the lives of husbands. This is a little secret that makes all the difference. As husbands, we are to give up our very lives for our wives, and yet what this passage is telling us is that every time we give up something for our wives, we benefit. When we sacrificially love our wives, we not only please

God, but whatever we do comes back to us as though we did it to ourselves. We cannot lose in this scenario; it is much like losing your life to follow Christ in order to gain it. If we hang onto our life, we end up losing it, but if we give it over to Christ, we gain it. If we give up our life for our wife, we actually will gain it back for our own benefit. God has got our backs, and He challenges us to trust Him in this truth. Love selfishly and gain nothing in return. Love sacrificially and gain a wealth of love from Christ Himself.

> *Old-book knowledge*: For whoever would save his life will lose it, but whoever loses his life for my sake and the gospel's will save it. (Mk 8:35, ESV)

The Mystery

The mystery is this: a man and a woman bonding into one flesh. But now, just to make it even more interesting, we see that God's blueprint for marriage is a pattern of a mystery; together, we represent Christ and His church. Paul explains, "This mystery is profound, and I am saying that it refers to Christ and the church." (Eph. 5:32, ESV). Not only has God given us a blueprint to follow in our marriage, but He has also given us an opportunity to represent Him in our marriage. If we do a good job of following His blueprint, we have the privilege of being His ambassadors. An ambassador represents his country within a foreign country. When foreigners speak to an ambassador, it is as if they are speaking directly to the citizens of his country. When foreigners attack or harm our ambassadors, it is as if they are attacking or harming us.

Why did terrorists recently attack and kill J. Christopher Stephens, our ambassador in Benghazi, Libya? Was it because they didn't like him? No, they probably didn't even know him; he just represented the United States. It is a privilege to represent Christ as ambassadors to His kingdom. If we do a poor job of following God's blueprint, we are disqualified and not capable of being his ambassadors, and we miss out on the honor of serving Him in this way. To represent something greater than yourself is an honor, and we should honor Mr. Stephens in laying down his life as a representative of this country. And we should strive to honor Christ in our marriage as representatives of His divine kingdom.

Ambassadors have an important job to do. As imitators of God, we are to model Christ and the church in our marriage. Our foundation is Christ and His Word. The husband assumes the role of Christ in loving his wife, and the wife assumes the role of the church in submitting to the leadership of her husband. Does this mean that the wife is not required to love her husband but only to submit to him? Is the husband only to love the wife and never submit to her? There is only one reference in the Bible where it speaks concerning the wife loving the husband, "And so train the young women to love their husbands and children." (Tit. 2:4, ESV), and there is no reference at all to the husband submitting to the wife. So what are we to think?

Remember, we must apply all of Scripture to our marriage, and throughout Scripture, we are commanded to love one another. "This is my commandment, that you love one another as I have loved you." (Jn 15:12, ESV). The wife cannot make an exception for her husband on this. Likewise, we are commanded to submit to one another as we just read in verse 21 of Ephesians chapter 5, and we cannot make an exception for the husband on this either.

I have had a few pastors disagree with me on this point. They say that Christ never submits to the church but is the head of the church, and similarly, that the husband should never submit to the wife but is the head of the wife. But I say when Christ made Himself lower than the angels to become a man and die for our sins that He submitted to us, the church. Paul explains, "And being found in human form, he humbled himself by becoming obedient to the point of death, even death on a cross!" (Phil. 2:8, ESV). Christ set the example of the leader who came to serve, to wash our feet, so that we would wash each other's feet, and thus He was leading us by example. When Christ washed the disciples' feet, it was an example of submission, when He took our sins on His shoulders, it was without a doubt submission to our need on behalf of the Father's will. Peter said to him, "You shall never wash my feet." Jesus answered him, "If I do not wash you, you have no share with me." (Jn 13:8, ESV).

In the Ephesian passage, the apostle Paul seems to be speaking more to our bents. He understood the real issues of marriage. Wives do not generally struggle with loving their husbands, but do struggle with respecting and submitting to them. This may be a result of the fall and the subsequent curse as recorded in Genesis. Genesis records the wife, "Your desire shall be for your husband, and he shall rule over you." (Gen. 3:16, ESV). This word *desire* here is not in the good sense. It is the same word that God used when speaking to Cain before he murdered his brother, Abel. God said, "If you do well, will you not be accepted? And if you do not do well, sin is crouching at the door. Its desire is for you, but you must rule over it." (Gen. 4:7, ESV). Doesn't this sound familiar? As part of the curse of the woman in a fallen world, she will desire to rule over her husband, but it will not happen, and we see throughout history how man has used his physical prowess over women in very unkind, domineering ways. Likewise, husbands do not generally struggle with submitting to their wives but with loving them. It's not unusual to hear a guy say, "Whatever she wants, just keep her happy, I don't want any trouble." This, too, may be a result of the fall and subsequent curse. This could be why in marriage, our struggle is often: women submitting and men loving. God's blueprinted design, however, calls for us to rise above our natural and fallen state in the way in which we conduct ourselves in marriage.

Simply put, the framework for our marriage becomes "love and respect." However, let each one of you love his wife as himself, and let the wife see that she respects her husband." (Ephesians 5:33). The apostle Paul summarizes his blueprint for marriage in this one verse, and he changes the word from *submit* to respect. He wants us to understand that the relationship between husband and wife is different than the relationship between church members when it comes to submitting and loving. The Greek word used here translated respect is *phobeo*, or fear or reverence, more than an act of obedience, but an attitude coming from the heart. The correlation here is the church's reverence for Christ, and the wife's respect of her husband. Therefore, it is no coincidence that the greatest need of men in marriage is honor coming from the respect they receive originating from their wives, and the greatest need of women in marriage is the love they receive originating from their husbands in the way they provide security and protection.

Building a precise godly framework is not always as easy as just following the blueprint. As we will see in the final chapters God has given us freedom in the execution of His design. With that freedom, we are expected to get all of the nuances of our building right. To accomplish this, we need to know and understand Him as the designer and what His vision is for the final product. For now, in the following chapter, we will focus on integrating our floor plan into our framework. The floor plan is essential to the functionality of what you're building and is key to understanding the purposes of the designer.

Questions for Group Discussion

- How will submitting to authorities in your life help your marriage?
- What are some of the challenges in following God's design with husbands as leaders?
- Why is the care and protection of the wife so important? What does it represent?
- How does independence damage marriage? What does dependence do for marriage?
- What are the implications of mutual love and respect in marriage?

4

The Floor Plan: DNA of Marriage

My wife Fran and I have been teaching a class for pre-married couples for over ten years now. The idea of dependence upon each other and becoming one as a couple has always been a key element in our teaching. Over time, we began to realize that marriage itself is creating something new that never existed before, much like the combining of DNA in our children to make up a new individual. DNA is a combination of bases that make up the vast differences in biological life. In analogy, understanding these bases will give us part of a blueprint helping us build a better marriage. The DNA of marriage becomes our floor plan.

DNA consists of two long polymer strands of simple units called nucleotides. These two strands run in opposite directions to each other and are anti-parallel. These strands have one of four types of molecules called bases that are attached to them. It is the sequence of these four nucleic bases along the backbone that encodes genetic information. Now, to use this analogy, we need to identify the two strands, and the four bases that make up our floor plan for marriage.

Strand One: Marriage Is Not a Religious Thing

There is something built into the core of our being that pushes us toward marriage. From an evolutionary standpoint, marriage doesn't make any sense; it seems to go beyond the realm of a simple tool used for females to eliminate unsuitable seed spreaders. What really stumps some sociologists is why marriage is still around, and how it seems to survive all human circumstances. Understanding marriage as a norm with physical, mental, and spiritual health implications should change our outlook. Is the blueprint for marriage actually built directly into our DNA? Old-book knowledge says yes. In his book, *The Marriage Problem: How Our Culture has Weakened Families*; James Wilson tries to make sense of it all:

> Marriage survives despite the absence of many sexual or economic reasons for it. Men and women will make public pledges of loyalty to one another even when both the man and the woman can buy sex on the marketplace and when women can use birth control or abortion to eliminate the chances of unwanted children and take advantage of educational opportunities and an open job market to make their own careers. Despite the apparent advantages of the single life, the desire for children and companionship is not a weak force among humans. The desire is found in most people, perhaps because human experience over the millennia have made such feelings a deep part of human emotions. Evolution has selected for sentiments that encourage marriage but not for those that require it.[3]

Evolution, like luck is not an actual entity, so you could say, "Luck has selected for sentiments that encourage marriage but not for those that require it." Whether you call it luck or evolution there is no designer or blueprint at work.

> *Old-book knowledge*: So the Lord God caused a deep sleep to fall upon the man, and while he slept took one of his ribs and closed up its place with flesh. And the rib that the Lord God had taken from the man he made into a woman and brought her to the man. (Gen. 2:21–22, ESV)

Strand Two: Marriage Is a Religious Thing

Understanding the role of religious influence in marriage is a complex matter, but few would argue that marriage isn't religious. Every religion has its views and customs attempting to influence marriage in some form. It has been my experience that even unreligious people still want religion when it comes to marriage. They want a pastor or minister of some kind to marry them. In some cases, they want to exchange vows and be married in a church, even if it's the first or last time they darken the door. Why haven't all marriages come to be defined as civil unions in our post-modern world? Why do we have an equality movement centered on marriage? If marriage as an institution isn't religious, then what legitimacy beyond legality are people seeking? It seems to be religiously planted into our very DNA.

> *Old-book knowledge*: But from the beginning of creation, "God made them male and female." "Therefore a man shall leave his father and mother and hold fast to his wife, and the two shall become one flesh." So they are no longer two but one flesh. What therefore God has joined together let not man separate. (Mk 10:6–9, ESV)

Base 1: Marriage Is Good Organization

If you had to come up with a new way to organize the communities around us, you couldn't come up with a better solution for organization than marriage. Marriage is the best way to provide for people economically and reduce poverty. Marriage is the best solution for a loving and stable environment for children to grow and develop. Marriage is the best solution for education. Most of the school teachers I have talked with say that their biggest problem in successfully teaching kids in their classrooms is lack of parental involvement. Communities with a large percentage of stable marriages seems to fare better against drugs, violence, and crime in general and there seems to be a direct correlation between marriage breakdown and poverty.[4]

> *Old-book knowledge*: And God blessed them. And God said to them, "Be fruitful and multiply and fill the earth and subdue it, and have dominion over the fish of the sea and over the birds of the heavens and over every living thing that moves on the earth." (Gen. 1:28, ESV)

Base 2: Marriage Is About Companionship

We sometimes get this wrong today. She has her friends and he has his friends and then there is their marriage. What makes this wrong is not having friends, but considering your friends as an emotional support system outside of and separate from your marriage, or, in some cases, even in competition with your marriage. Today, couples are getting married at increasingly older ages and usually each individual has already established some kind of support system as a single through friends and close relatives and work and school associates. When an individual has a well-established support system in place before marriage, it can lead to difficulties in establishing a spouse as a primary companion, and companionship or friendship is one of the key indicators of success in marriage. In his book, *The Seven Principles for Making Marriage Work*, John Gottman states, "At the heart of my program is the simple truth that happy marriages are based on deep friendship. By this I mean a mutual respect for and enjoyment of each other's company."[5]

I am not saying that you can't have friends outside of your marriage, but what I am saying is that if your friends are fulfilling the primary companionship role in your life, it won't help you have a good marriage. In other words, if your friends get upset and don't support you, or they get mad and leave you, or they just leave you for other reasons like moving away or passing away, you may be sad, but you won't be derailed because your primary need is being met by your spouse. Remember, this is your marriage DNA at work: spouses are to be companions. It is in the blueprint.

> *Old-book knowledge*: Then the Lord God said, "It is not good that the man should be alone; I will make him a helper fit for him." (Gen. 2:18, ESV)

Base 3: Marriage Creates a New Unit

Parents keep out. Most parents do have life-long relationships with their children, but when they interject themselves, or are allowed to interject themselves into their children's marriage, it doesn't work. Marriage needs to be the creation of a new unit of organization. Parents may have a life-long relationship, but it is unnatural and not ideal for a parent to be a life-long companion. Only marriage works well for this type of intimacy. I am not saying that parents, like friends, can't have a role in your life, but what I am saying is, if they have too much of a role interfering with your spousal relationship, you won't have the satisfying, high-performance, blueprinted marriage that you crave.

> *Old-book knowledge*: He who finds a wife finds a good thing and obtains favor from the Lord. (Prov. 18:22, ESV)

Base 4: Marriage Is about Sex

I've heard that sex oftentimes ruins a perfectly good friendship. Why should this be the case, especially if friendship is the best way to be successful in marriage? It all goes back to our DNA, sex is the best relationship-building tool that a couple has at their disposal for building mutual trust, respect, and enjoyment, but without the unwavering commitment that marriage should be based on, sex ends up becoming a land mine that explodes on us. There is a difference between a friendship that grows into a life-long commitment and one that begins with a life-long commitment. Commitment is the X factor in sexual fulfillment. I know this is not a popular idea within our culture today. We spend a lot of money convincing people that sex is just what consenting adults do for fun, and marriage is something different, not really about sex, but according to the blueprint, sex is what marriage is all about.

Current studies show that the number of couples getting married today is at a lower ratio than ever before in the history of our nation.[6]

The importance of marriage and the pursuit of marriage and family commitment declines when sex is readily available without marriage. The importance of marriage, the pursuit of marriage and a desire for family commitment increases when sex becomes an exclusive activity within marriage. We can see this dynamic at work when investigating population ratios of men and women and the affect it has on marriages.[7]

Looking at the birth rates of unwed mothers, the number of marriages, and loose family connections, it is not that hard to correlate them to population ratios of men and women, but population ratios just highlight the real connection found in the overall attitude of sex. Where women outnumber men, marriage becomes somewhat outdated and unimportant; sex is generally not exclusive to marriage, and the opposite is true in societies where men outnumber women, allowing women to demand commitment among other things before sex. Our attitude about sex, which is no longer just affected by population, affects our view of marriage, family, and meaningful relationships.

> *Old-book knowledge*: But because of the temptation to sexual immorality, each man should have his own wife and each woman her own husband. (1 Cor. 7:2, ESV)

Go with a Blueprint

- Realize the mental, emotional, and spiritual benefits of a healthy marriage.
- Organize your life around your marriage.
- Cultivate friendship and companionship with your spouse.
- Create a new family unit with your marriage.
- Use sex exclusively in marriage as a relationship-building tool.

Counselor's Notes

God's blueprint design for marriage is limited by God's DNA code for marriage, but limitless in the way they are combined into relationships as individual couples. Therefore, when a couple is joined together in holy matrimony, God creates something that has never existed before as a whole new DNA sequence. What, therefore, God has joined together let not man separate (Mark 10:9). Of course, when it comes to theology, all analogies eventually breakdown and this is just meant to provide us a picture to work with not a scientifically accurate correlation.

Strand 1: Explained

The New Testament Scriptures and the old Hebrew Scriptures come together representing the DNA strands or backbone of the marriage relationship. Strand one, the theology of marriage as represented by the old Hebrew Scriptures upholds marriage as divinely ordained, a mysterious and symbolic union. "So the Lord God caused a deep sleep to fall upon the man, and while he slept took one of his ribs and closed up its place with flesh. And the rib that the Lord God had taken from the man he made into a woman and brought her to the man." (Gen. 2:21, ESV). Why did God create the woman in this fashion? Why didn't he just speak her into existence like the heaven and earth? Why didn't he form her from the dust of the ground like Adam? Why didn't he just create the woman and give her to Adam? Why did he feel it necessary to perform the very first surgery on Adam when he created the woman, Eve? He created the woman this way for one reason and one reason only. He wanted to show us the special relationship that he was creating between a man and woman in marriage. He wanted to show us a picture of oneness that he envisioned for the marriage relationship. We have a God that has revealed himself in the pages of his word as a God rich in symbolism. Our God is very symbolic, and he uses symbolism to teach us things about himself and us and the world around us that he created.

The story from Joshua 4 always has me contemplating the notion of rock piles.

> Then Joshua called the twelve men from the people of Israel, whom he had appointed, a man from each tribe. And Joshua said to them, "Pass on before the ark of the Lord your God into the midst of the Jordan, and take up each of you a stone upon his shoulder, according to the number of the tribes of the people of Israel, that this may be a sign among you. When your children

ask in time to come, 'What do those stones mean to you?'" (Josh. 4:4–6, ESV)

God is always symbolically piling up rocks to garner our attention of what he is trying to accomplish in our life. Much like trusting and waiting for his provision and looking back on his providence as we seek out his will for our life. Yes, we have a very symbolic God, and if he went to the trouble to give us a picture of marriage that we can't forget, then we shouldn't ignore it. Marriage is God's design and God's institution, and there is no doubt that God takes our marriages more seriously than we do. Marriage was not just a token gesture from God toward man, but marriage was part and parcel to his overall creative design of man from the beginning.

Strand 1: Confirmed

This divinely ordained, mysterious, and symbolic union is confirmed by Christ to be the union of one man to one woman.

> And Pharisees came up to him and tested him by asking, "Is it lawful to divorce one's wife for any cause?" He answered, "Have you not read that he who created them from the beginning made them male and female, and said, 'Therefore a man shall leave his father and his mother and hold fast to his wife, and the two shall become one flesh'? So they are no longer two but one flesh. What therefore God has joined together let not man separate." (Matt. 19:3–6, ESV)

You've probably heard it said that if the Bible says something once, it's worth paying attention to, but if the Bible says something more than once, we probably ought to really sit up and pay attention. This picture of marriage as described first in Genesis as an inspired insertion is seen in the Bible four times. The Lord Jesus Christ confirms it again in the Gospel of Mark:

But from the beginning of creation, "God made them male and female." "Therefore a man shall leave his father and mother and hold fast to his wife, and the two shall become one flesh." So they are no longer two but one flesh. What therefore God has joined together let not man separate. (Mk 10:6–9, ESV)

Men can decide to define marriage in any way they please, but this does not mean that God will ever change his mind about marriage. The State of California and other governments can decide to make marriage valid between men and men and women and women or two men and two women or any combination, thereof, but marriage is a creation of God, and as such, He defines it, He ordains it, He decides its purpose, and He gives us a workable blueprint to live it out in a way that is pleasing to him. Rebelling against God's design for marriage is no more or no less egregious than rebelling against any of God's principles for our lives. Like most architects that have mastered a design and created a blueprint, God is not pleased when we build something that does not reflect what he intended for us to build.

Strand 1: Permanent

Another characteristic of this old Hebrew strand is the idea of permanence. The divinely ordained, mysterious, and symbolic union is meant to be sacred and binding. "It was also said, 'Whoever divorces his wife, let him give her a certificate of divorce.' But I say to you that everyone who divorces his wife, except on the ground of sexual immorality, makes her commit adultery, and whoever marries a divorced woman commits adultery." (Matt. 5:31–32, ESV)

For the man who does not love his wife but divorces her, says the Lord, the God of Israel, covers his garment with violence, says the Lord of hosts, so guard yourselves in your spirit, and do not be faithless. (Mal. 2:16, ESV)

Here in Matthew, Jesus is not trying to establish a new set of rules and order for divorce and remarriage, but he is merely pointing out the heart of God and his longing for permanence when it comes to marriage. He understands the situations of fallen men that lead to divorce, but he wants us to understand that it was never part of his perfect plan for us. When it comes to marriage, he wants us to have a heart for him, and that heart will have an attitude of faithfulness and lifelong commitment to our partner in marriage. We see His emphasis on the heart in another statement, claiming that lusting in the heart alone equates to adultery. "But I say to you that everyone who looks at a woman with lustful intent has already committed adultery with her in his heart." (Matt. 5:28, ESV). Man looks on the outward, but God is continually looking inward, and he seeks those that would have a heart for him not just an outward display of stylized behavior.

In Malachi, God prophesies to us concerning the result of not looking at marriage as sacred and binding. He says that our garments will be filled with violence. When you go outside to walk at night, what neighborhood do you want to walk in? The neighborhood lined with houses filled with two-parent homes for their kids, or the neighborhood with single or no-parent homes and unloved and unsupervised kids? The neighborhood filled with loving marriages, or the neighborhood filled with no marriages or broken marriages? If this example doesn't ring true to you, you probably live a somewhat sheltered life, or you're not being emotionally and intellectually honest, or you're just being obstinate against my view.

I worked as a UPS driver for many years, and I also worked into the night on many occasions. I didn't have to think twice about my answer. The truth is that much of the violence in our society, and I understand that this is a stereotype and there are always exceptions, can be attributed to angry young males who are products of sex. There is much to discuss concerning the interpretation of this passage in Malachi, but it would be a stretch to find favor against this first DNA strand of God's blueprint. God understands the seriousness of not following marriage by his design, and His design remains unchanged.

Strand 1: Procreate

A third characteristic of the first strand is that God's union is designed to procreate godly children. Did he not make them one, with a portion of the Spirit in their union? And this oneness God seeks results in what? A union that brings forth godly offspring, "So guard yourselves in your spirit, and let none of you be faithless to the wife of your youth." (Mal. 2:15, ESV). If we would all just do a good job of passing our faith on to our children, we wouldn't really need any other evangelism in the church. God's design was to multiply faith from generation to generation. This could only be accomplished by godly marriages perpetuating godly families. God sent the flood to destroy Cainitic evil in the world. Cain represented the breakdown of godly familial life that could sustain the message of the savior from generation to generation. Cain's rebellion hit right to the heart of what we now call the gospel message—God wanted to perpetuate this message throughout the generations. The sacrificial system that Cain refused to acknowledge was a sacred symbolism of the coming Lamb of God who would take away the sin of the world. God wanted men to experience firsthand the injustice of brutally putting to death an innocent lamb. This first official organized attempt by Satan to snuff out God's testimony on earth resulted in the destruction of all flesh, except Noah and his family. Eve was not just thankful for another son, but another son that would carry the seed. The seed being the godly message preserved in the world. Eventually, the seed would come to represent the gospel message or good news of Jesus Christ, the Messiah. Evidently, it is God's love for us that motivates him to interject into our free will, so that we don't leave ourselves without a testimony or knowledge of Him, and His plan for our undeserving redemption.

Post-flood attempts to quench the God story in the world were led by Nimrod, the mighty hunter. We could call his organized, satanic plan the Babylonian evil.

> Then they said, "Come, let us build ourselves a city and
> a tower with its top in the heavens, and let us make a

name for ourselves, lest we be dispersed over the face of the whole earth." (Gen. 11:4, ESV)

God's plan was for men to be fruitful and multiply and fill the earth. Nimrod's plan was to congregate in a great society where evil influences would eventually destroy the God story preserved by God through man. Keep all of your apples in one basket, and then introduce a bad apple to spoil the bunch. God slowed down this system by introducing language barriers that would force man into filling the earth and scattering abroad. A commandment they were ignoring at the time.

This Babylonian evil is still at work in the world today in the form of false religion. Nimrod's initial version was squashed, but the evil of corrupting influence continues on to this present day, making the need for godly marriages that produce godly children to carry the testimony to the world all that more crucial to God's design and blueprint for your marriage. You see, God has a greater purpose and value for your marriage than you give Him credit for. Abraham fathered the godly nation that was a peculiar people, holy, and set apart by God. Why? Because it is primary to God's plan to advance God followers who continue to perpetuate the God story in a world of corrupted influences. The nation of Israel carried the story till the time of Christ, and then, their peculiar customs, once influential in serving the Lord, became part of the corrupting influence of the Babylonian evil that had to be squashed once again. Now, His church carries the torch to preserve the testimony among the nations against increasingly tough, anti-Christian influences. For the mystery of lawlessness is already at work. "Only he who now restrains it will do so until he is out of the way." (2 Thess. 2:7, ESV). Today, this evil is in the process of transforming from a system of wide–spread, false religions to a syncretistic system of religious faith, which will include all forms of secular humanism. And on her forehead was written a name of mystery:

> Babylon the great, mother of prostitutes and of earth's abominations. These are of one mind, and they hand over their power and authority to the beast. They will make war on the Lamb, and the Lamb will conquer

them, for he is Lord of lords and King of kings, and those with him are called and chosen and faithful. (Rev. 17:5, 13–14, ESV)

This current strain of Babylonian evil will ultimately be squashed, but first, it will enjoy another glory period, as in the days of Nimrod. It may well be that God's Spirit working in and through the hearts of those unified in His church body, led by godly marriages and families, are the only restraining influence in the world today. Raising godly children is still a key part of God's overall strategy for keeping evil influences in the world at bay. He hasn't changed his mind, though the enemy continues to morph his designs and strategies against Him.

Today's form of Babylonian evil will not be the final attempt by Satan to eliminate the God story among the nations. Revelation gives a brief glimpse into a future strategy of Satan.

And when the thousand years are ended, Satan will be released from his prison and will come out to deceive the nations that are at the four corners of the earth, Gog and Magog, to gather them for battle; their number is like the sand of the sea. (Rev. 20:7–8, ESV)

We could call this new and final strategy of Satan: Gog and Magog evil. The destruction of all evil flesh, just like in the days of Noah, will precede this final attempt of Satan to rid the world of the God story. In a perfect world ruled by Christ himself, where the population has soared like the sand of the sea—it only seems logical that Satan's focus will be on the children of those that entered into the rest of God's earthly kingdom. Like Noah, those who witnessed the total destruction of evil are not at risk, but were saved out of the destruction into God's rest, or ark, if you will. If they fail to keep the God story alive from generation to generation through godly influences—their children will be at risk, amazingly, even living in a perfect world like Adam and Eve, many will rebel. Satan will still be deceiving and men and women will still choose his lies over God. So it appears that raising godly children with a heart to follow God will be just as important in the final days as it was in the past and as it is in the present. If your marriage is not capable of perpetuating the God story, it is corrupting God's blueprint in a significant way. How much more important is our marriage to God than it is to us? The fate of many may rest on the godly testimony that your relationship can provide if designed after God's plan and purpose for your marriage.

Stand 2: Unconditional Love

Now, let's turn our focus to the second strand in the DNA of marriage. This New Testament strand depicts the mysterious union of marriage as a representation of Christ and His church. "Therefore a man shall leave his father and mother and hold fast to his wife, and the two shall become one flesh." (Eph. 5:31–32, ESV). This mystery is profound, and I am saying that it refers to Christ and the church. Here the apostle Paul gives us brand-new insight into a new purpose for marriage. God has not changed his mind about marriage, but we now have a fuller understanding of God's ultimate purpose for marriage in light of Christ's contribution to the redemption of fallen men. So the first and only point under this second strand is that God's union is an unconditional covenant relationship.

> Behold, the days are coming, declares the Lord, when I will make a new covenant with the house of Israel and the house of Judah, not like the covenant that I made with their fathers on the day when I took them by the hand to bring them out of the land of Egypt, my covenant that they broke, though I was their husband, declares the Lord. (Jer. 31:31–32, ESV)

You see, God has always looked at his relationship with men much like a marriage. The oneness that he designed from the beginning was always an intentional reflection of the relationship he desires with us.

In the Hebrew Scriptures, under the law, we had what are known as suzerainty covenants. Suzerainty covenants are if-then covenants, or contracts that say, "If you do this, then I will do this." If you will obey me and follow my commandments, then I will bless you. If you disobey Me, I will pull my blessing from you.

> You yourselves have seen what I did to the Egyptians, and how I bore you on eagles' wings and brought you to myself. Now therefore, if you will indeed obey my voice and keep my covenant, you shall be my treasured possession among all peoples, for all the earth is mine; and you shall be to me a kingdom of priests and a holy nation. These are the words that you shall speak to the people of Israel. (Exod. 19:4–6, ESV)

The sovereign power, God, lays out the terms for continuing relationship. "But if you will not obey the voice of the Lord your God or be careful to do all his commandments and His statutes that I command you today, then all these curses shall come upon you and overtake you." (Deut. 28:15, ESV).

In this second strand, it is revealed that marriage is to be based on a covenant of unity and not sovereignty. We now have a more complete picture of the new covenant that was created in Christ's blood. And he took bread, and when he had given thanks, he broke it and gave it to them, saying, "This is my body, which is given for you. Do this in remembrance of me." And likewise, the cup after they had eaten, saying, "This cup that is poured out for you is the new covenant in my blood." (Lk 22:19–20, ESV).

This new covenant in Christ's blood is an unconditional covenant. Christ has revealed that He loves us and gave Himself for us, even though we broke covenant with Him, now we have unconditional acceptance through His unbreakable blood covenant, as long as we willingly believe and enter into that covenant. This is why the old-fashioned marriage vows are written the way that they are. These vows represent Christ's unconditional love for us, and his desire that we model His love in our marriage—for better or for worse, for richer or for poorer, in sickness and in health, until death do us part. Nowadays, many couples prefer to write their own vows, which is okay, but if I am performing their ceremony, I require that they do the traditional vows as well because they are meant to set a standard of how marriage should be a reflection of Christ and His church.

We have now set the strands for this little DNA of marriage theological analogy, so now let's take a look at the bases that connect these strands. In real DNA, the bases are adenine, thymine, guanine, and cytosine. The bases remain the same, but the combination of their structure within the strands is what leads to unique coding possibilities. Likewise, the theological bases determined for marriage will be relational building precursors for every marriage, but at the same time, will reveal uniqueness in the structure and manifestation of the marriage relationship.

Base 1: Organization

Base one: marriage is God's design for order and community. And God blessed them. And God said to them, "Be fruitful and multiply and fill the earth and subdue it, and have dominion over the fish of the sea and over the birds of the heavens and over every living thing that moves on the earth." (Gen. 1:28, ESV). Notice that God didn't say, "Adam, govern the earth and rule over it, Oh, and by the way, here's Eve to help you." He said to them, "Fill the earth and govern it." The marriage relationship was God's first unit of organization in the world. This is likely why societies and governments that promote marriage as one of the key units of organization and leadership will tend to be more prosperous as they reap benefits from God's original creative design. Likewise, those societies that refuse to elevate God's design in their societal order will likely suffer counter-productivity and failure.

Wilson argues from his research findings that the breakdown in marriage is hurting our modern society in many ways; including education, teen pregnancies, financial instability, emotional stress, drug use, and crime. Wilson argues that the most salient way to rebuild and strengthen society is to return to having a solid marital structure at its core.[8]

His findings, regardless of how you view the statistical relevancy of his elements, agree with the biblical blueprint for order and community, with marriage being the essential unit of God's design.

It is no surprise, based on God's Word, that strong marriages promote strong governments, strong organizations, and strong communities. Support of marriage based on God's design is a good baseline for leadership strategy at any level.

Base 2: Companionship

Base two: marriage is God's provision for companionship. Then the Lord God said, "It is not good that the man should be alone; I will make him a helper fit for him." (Gen. 2:18, ESV). "Enjoy life with the wife whom you love, all the days of your vain life that he has given you under the sun, because that is your portion in life and in your toil at which you toil under the sun." (Eccl. 9:9, ESV). This is what God wants for us by design. He wants you to follow His solution for companionship. His plan calls for your spouse to be your primary source of companionship, so when you have your companionship needs being met by someone other than your spouse, you're living contrary to God's design, and it will lead to difficulty in your marriage. It is unhealthy to have a friend, sibling, or even a parent fulfilling a companionship role in your life that God has assigned to your spouse, and it is also unhealthy to ignore your responsibilities as a companion to your spouse, forcing an ungodly relationship attachment to others, even children in our life.

Base 3: New Priority

Base three: marriage creates a new authority and priority. Your children cannot be a primary source of companionship because God wants them to eventually leave your sphere of influence. When a person gets married, God no longer wants them to be under the authority of their parents, but he wants a completely new unit to be established. Remember, God's design for order and community is based on the marriage unit, and he wants new units established all of the time. We do more harm than good when we ignore this base, and we make natural transitions more difficult as well.

Sometimes, couples struggle with this when they attempt to set up a new authority and priority because they get confused with their mandate to honor their parents. Honoring your parents does not mean that you are still under their authority. The highest honor you can bestow on your parents is to be a godly man or godly woman. If your son grows up to be POTUS, President of the United States, that bestows honor onto you for raising a child who accomplished such a feat, but being a godly person is far more honor to your parents than being an important person by worldly standards. Therefore, there is absolutely no higher honor you can give your parents than to become a godly person.

Parents, beware of trying to yield too much influence in your children's lives as adults. Of course, we are all to yield godly influence toward each other in the church. "And let us consider how to stir up one another to love and good works." (Heb. 10:24, ESV). But God wants the authority to change upon marriage, and we would do well to honor this design. This issue of parental influence within the marriage relationship is one that is frequented in counseling. One must distance oneself from the former parent-child relationship in order to make sound, godly decisions when it comes to working through problems. This is true in both the parents' and the adult child's perspectives.

Another conclusion that can be entertained as we look at parent-and-adult-child relationships from God's blueprinted perspective is that parental authority changes only upon marriage and not based on some arbitrary age or individual status. We have set eighteen as the age of an adult in our communities, but parents will sometimes override society's age norm by invoking some arbitrary status like financial independence as the determinate of authority change. Neither of these appear to be supported by scripture, though both may have some merit when it comes to legitimizing marriage.

We have a cultural aversion to authority, but God has no such aversion. "Let every person be subject to the governing authorities. For there is no authority except from God, and those that exist have been instituted by God." (Rom. 13:1, ESV). It might seem unreasonable to us that we should remain under our parents' authority until marriage, especially when we are legally adults and financially independent, but that seems to be God's standard. Of course, being under your parents' authority when you are older and financially independent may look a little different than otherwise, but either way, it seems to be an attitude of submission and respect more so than a legalistic enforcement. Of course, God's authority in our life trumps all others in any circumstance. But Peter and the apostles answered, "We must obey God rather than men." (Acts 5:29, ESV). There may be fine points that could be argued, but marriage is God's unit of organization, and as such, it not only establishes authority in our life, but it helps us to develop priority in life as well. God hasn't changed his mind, and he doesn't offer us a plan B. In the real world, we tend to go with plan B more often than plan A, but that is because of our natural tendency to get it wrong the first time. God doesn't need a do-over. His plan A is always right. "There is a way that seems right to a man, but its end is the way to death." (Prov. 14:12, ESV). We will benefit from observing His plan A.

Base 4: Sex

Base four: marriage is God's only provision for sexual activity. "But because of the temptation to sexual immorality, each man should have his own wife and each woman her own husband." (1 Cor. 7:2, ESV). Yes, God made us sexual beings, and then he said, "Oh, by the way, there is only one way you can honor me in this and that is to practice sex exclusively in a committed marriage relationship." Sexual activity is not just reserved for creating children, but it is also intended for the mutual pleasure of the husband and wife. "Let your fountain be blessed, and rejoice in the wife of your youth." (Prov. 5:18, ESV).

In God's blueprint for marriage, relationship and sex are one in the same. God never intended for sex to be something that consenting adults participate in just for fun, outside of the context of marriage. Sex is one of the best relationship tools that God has given us for a very close one-to-one flesh bonded connection, and as such, is a very important strand to the DNA of marriage.

Recapping—the theological DNA of marriage consists of two strands. Strand one: marriage is a divinely ordained and mysterious, symbolic union. Strand two: this divinely ordained, mysterious and symbolic union now depicts Christ and His church. God designed marriage as a key element in worldly order and general community,

His main provision for companionship, the beginning of a new authority and priority in life, and our only provision for sexual activity. How we live out these purposes may look somewhat different in each and every marriage, but the elements available in His blueprint are the same for all men in all locations and in all ages, past, present, and future. God's DNA for marriage calls for the same building blocks universally, anything more or less is merely a mutation of God's design.

Questions for Group Discussion

- How will a healthy marriage benefit your life?
- How can you organize your life around marriage? How does a society organize itself around marriage?
- How can you cultivate companionship in your marriage?
- How are parental and extended family relationships affecting your marriage?
- What does it look like to practice sex as part of relationship?

5

Legend: How to Relate

Learning to read blueprints is essential for builders, planners, organizers, and cost analyzers. Blueprints generally have architectural and engineering scales to help us understand the dimensions of the project. Along with the scales come frequently used symbols representing various components of the building or project, and a legend explaining the meaning of each symbol for ease of reading. The legend deciphers the symbols, and as the reader becomes more and more familiar with the symbols and their representations, the legend becomes unnecessary. In our marriage blueprint, we need a legend to decipher the personality traits of our spouse. Often, our ability to read each other is hindered by our limited understanding of individual personality traits. Imagine how messed up a construction project could get when the plumber sees a shower stall where the electrician sees an electrical panel. Without guidance, we get confused because our mind's eye can see things quite differently from the way others see things.

Almost forty years ago, a well-known author, Tim Lahaye, wrote a book titled, *Spirit Controlled Temperament.*[9]

I was in high school at the time I began reading this book. I was so intrigued to learn of the four basic temperaments or personalities that people share. Human behavior has been a topic of interest for me ever since. We can use knowledge of individual personalities as an excuse for bad behavior in marriage, or we can take this knowledge and use it to help accentuate our personality strengths not defaulting to our personality weaknesses. Actually, it can be very important to understand personality traits; it not only helps us to identify our own strengths and weaknesses, but it teaches us how to relate to others, especially our own spouse.

The Real You: Temperament

Your temperament is a combination of inborn traits that subconsciously affect your behavior. The controversy surrounding the science of personalities revolves around the age-old question, "Are we products of our environment or are we just born with certain inclinations?" This is the whole nature versus nurture issue. Let me just say that after having three boys of my own, I am totally convinced that we are born with a personality DNA programmed right into us. Just like we have certain color hair and certain color eyes and a defined skin type and a distinctly shaped nose, we have a personality given to us, and we are wired that way by our Creator. It was apparent to me that my boys came right out of the womb with certain God-given characteristics in their temperament.

My oldest son, Carl, was born with a temperament almost identical to his grandfather. It was almost a surreal experience raising him when it came to coping with his personality. All of the personality conflicts that I had with my own dad growing up I now experienced in reverse as the father, not the son. Fortunately, I grew to respect and admire some of my dad's traits that were different from my own. My middle son, Casey, with his melancholy traits, resembled my own personality somewhat. I intuitively knew how to parent him because I understood his need to be involved in many different things and his desire not to draw attention to himself. My youngest son, Cary, is a lot like his phlegmatic mother, happy-go-lucky, unpressured, and easy to relate to. Unfortunately, I am the only one in the family with a tendency toward obsessive compulsive disorder and surviving the never-ending attack on my belongings and preferred life's motto, "A place for everything and everything in its place," had to be tempered with my family's motto, "A place for everything and everything all over the place." Of course, my oldest, as an adult, has developed more along the organized side of his temperament, but not until he started a household of his own. I could have used him on my side earlier on, oh well!

The Spiritual You: Character

Your character is the soul of you, being real with yourself, your mind, your emotions, and your will. Character is temperament affected by childhood training, education, beliefs, principles, and internal and external motivations. Your character is what religion is in the business of changing. Character defines who you are when nobody is watching. If you will steal when nobody is around and the cameras are off, then that says something about your character, but if you will not steal even when nobody is watching, then that says something different about your character. A person with good moral character understands or believes that performing for the crowd isn't what matters most.

> *Old-book knowledge*: Do not be conformed to this world, but be transformed by the renewal of your mind, that by testing you may discern what is the will of God, what is good and acceptable and perfect. (Rom. 12:2, ESV)

The Visible You: Persona

Your personality or persona is the public face that you put on, not necessarily revealing your true character. We generally refer to temperament, character, and personality all as personality, but your persona is actually an attempt to follow a human formula for accepted conduct. Sometimes, we use our personality as an excuse for bad behavior, especially in marriage. We say things like, "That's just the way I am, deal with it." Or, "You knew I was like this when you married me." In worst-case scenarios, people marry a persona and then are sorely confused and disappointed when the person they are married to is like a stranger.

> *Old-book knowledge*: Therefore, if anyone is in Christ, he is a new creation. The old has passed away; behold, the new has come. (2 Cor. 5:17, ESV)

Examining the Legend

A couple of years ago, my wife and I met with a couple to discuss their marital issues. They were newlyweds of only a couple of weeks at the time. Once we got them in the office, our necks got sore just watching them argue about various things back and forth and back and forth. After about thirty minutes of this dialogue, it became very apparent to me that they had a failure to relate to each other's personalities. She was an off-the-chart sanguine, and he was an off-the-chart phlegmatic. She wanted to socialize with friends and go and go and go, and he wanted to kick back and pop the top on his beer can and watch TV. I asked them to take a personality assessment and schedule an appointment to come back and discuss their results. He threw the assessment back at me and said, "I don't go in for all of that psychological mumbo jumbo!" I said, "Okay," and sent them on their way. Two weeks later, they were back in the office, going back and forth on the exact same futile discussion that they were having before. I stopped them and said, "Let me explain one thing to you—your wife has an off-the-charts sanguine personality, which means that if you want to be able to relate to her, you are going to have to have to throw her an occasional bone, and say, 'That sounds like a great idea, let's go to the beach and meet our friends for dinner!' and she is going to have to occasionally say, 'Let's just stay home tonight and kick back.' You're going to have to show some occasional enthusiasm, and she's going to have to mellow out in order for you to feel better about each other, and the relationship." At that point he said, "Well, go ahead and give me that assessment thing and we'll try it out and see what happens."

The study of personality and temperaments began with Hippocrates way back in 450 BC and continued with Galen in AD 190. The four basic personalities include melancholy, sanguine, phlegmatic, and choleric. Currently, large shares of the studies in personality are performed at the University of Minnesota. You may have heard of the MMPI, which stands for the Minnesota Multiphasic Personality Inventory. This is a widely used personality assessment and is very sophisticated in its understandings of how people lie and are dishonest on their personality profiles. If you turned up in a cornfield one day and started telling people that you had been abducted by aliens and taken into their spaceship and probed, some psychologist might give you the MMPI, and after an interview, determine the probability of your stretching the truth a bit. If you were to apply for some public service position, they might give you the MMPI to determine how suitable you are for a particular job with a particular set of responsibilities.

In marriage, understanding each other's basic temperament traits gives us a clear path to develop better skills at relating to each other, and thus, have a more harmonious relationship. Of course, opposites do attract, but when it comes to marriage, the more you have in common personality–wise, the less contentious the relationship. So we want to take a look at the four basic personalities and see how they react in marriage. With this information, we can learn how to be around each other, how to explain things to each other, how to support each other, how to recognize each other's needs, the proper way to talk with each other, the best way to work together, a preferred way to behave, what questions to ask, and how to cope with each other's weaknesses. Marita Littauer in her book, *Wired That Way*,[10] does an excellent job of elaborating on the four personality styles first introduced to me by Tim LaHaye. I also use her personality assessment tool[11] in counseling and marriage classes. We need to have a good understanding of how those styles will affect our ability to follow the blueprint in marriage, much like referring to a legend when you don't quite understand what you're dealing with when you see it right in front of you.

Sanguine: Let the Good Times Roll

The sanguine personality creates a marriage that is focused on fun. The sanguine is your popular people person and is usually the one in the room that everybody knows and everybody likes and everybody is attracted to. The sanguine is never at a loss for words and usually wants to speak now and think later. The sanguine is the most outgoing and extroverted temperament, and many people become jealous of the sanguine's ability to attract attention and communicate to others. If you think of the character, Tigger, in the cartoon, *Winnie the Pooh*, he reminds me of the sanguine personality. The sanguine personality will bring spontaneity, enthusiasm, flexibility, and compassion into your marriage. They will be good parents that spend a great deal of time playing with the kids, because they still are one. The sanguine personality will harm your marriage by drawing attention to themselves, sometimes inappropriately, which, along with being messy, overly dramatic, and spending money vicariously without a plan can put some strain on the marriage relationship to say the least.

Choleric: Get 'er Done

The choleric personality creates a marriage that is always on the go. The choleric is very ambitious and has no tolerance for aimless activity. The choleric is your basic what we call Type A personality. This is your natural-born leader who thrives on pressure, chooses sides, and does not care what anybody else thinks. When I picture a choleric in my mind, I see Donald Trump in that reality TV show, *The Apprentice*, where he made famous the phrase, "You're fired." The choleric personality will bring to marriage a respectful attitude, lots of energy, and a "my way or the highway" type of leadership. Cholerics are tough parents, hard to please, and very controlling. They will have a hard time with family commitments because they are generally career–oriented, and they are definitely not the touchy-feely type when it comes to relationships.

Melancholy: Give It Some Thought

The melancholy personality creates a marriage that is neat and orderly. Melancholies are generally thinkers and perfectionists. They are the most introverted of the temperaments and are prone to depression, thus the term, *melancholy*. Because the melancholy temperament is so analytical, they are prone to scientific and academic discovery, great artistry, and creative invention. When I think of melancholy, I think of Albert Einstein or Michelangelo Buonarrati, appreciated for their insights but harder to relate to on a personal level. The melancholy personality brings to marriage commitment and stability and long-term devotion. They are loving parents, but can become overly critical, overly routine, and they can hurt the marriage by having high expectations that, when left unmet, cause depression. When my wife, Fran, describes my melancholy personality traits, she loves to tell stories about my thirteen-column financial records and my tedious routines, like always having my shoes on when everybody else is dressed down and ready to relax before bed. She almost taunts me when describing how she and the boys used my scissors off of my desk and never returned them, becoming amused at my reaction and stress. They even went so far as to buy me a pack of about twenty scissors for my birthday one year, none of which can be located to this day. With melancholies, it's the small things and the big things, but it's always something that they're worried about.

Phlegmatic: Chill Out

The phlegmatic creates a marriage that is relaxed and easygoing. Phlegmatics have a way of never letting their feathers get ruffled or at least to appear as though their feathers never get ruffled. Phlegmatics are easy-going, but underneath, they are very worried about their own personhood and, therefore, can have a lot of hidden emotions. Phlegmatics like to kick back and watch other people, and they are usually very intelligent, and when you combine those two traits, it makes them great at practical jokes and timing when it comes to humor. If you have ever watched the TV show, *The Office*, Jim in that series is the quintessential phlegmatic. He is not very driven to lead or develop special projects, but he is very efficient at his job and well aware of everything else that is going on in the office with his coworkers. He can find the humor in all situations and orchestrate people into that humor.

The phlegmatic personality brings to marriage dependability and agreeableness. They are very patient and modest and make good parents. They can hurt a marriage by being poor communicators; passive aggressive with little motivation to change, and it can be said that if two phlegmatics get married, they will never go anywhere. My wife, Fran, is a high phlegmatic, and she calls herself "The

66

Sniper," meaning she lets things build up inside of her, and when you least expect it, she'll take you out at the knees. There were times I never knew what hit me. But, all in all, I usually say that if you can't be married to a phlegmatic, you can't be married to anyone.

Mix It Up

Discovering the temperament of people around you will not only help you to relate better in marriage, but it will also help you to relate better to people in all kinds of circumstances. For instance, if your boss is a choleric and you have a report that is due on Friday, he would be impressed if you turned the report in on Thursday. You, on the other hand, may be a melancholy and able to turn that report in on Thursday, but you would have to fight back the urge to cross all of your T's and dot all of your I's. Of course, as a melancholy, you will turn the report in on time and it will be perfect, but this will not impress your boss. Now if you turn the report in on Thursday, in your mind, you have not done a good job and have turned in a substandard report, but your choleric boss does not care about perfection, and he or she will be impressed with the early report. He might say something like, "I wasn't so sure about that, Gary, but now I'm beginning to think that he is developing into a very good employee." You see, you have taken into account your boss's personality, and now, you are relating to him in a positive way.

To understand how the four personalities might interact with each other, we could use the example of a building committee at your church. The choleric on the building committee would just ask: "What do you want built? Get out of the way and I will build it for you." In other words, what is the task at hand? The sanguine on the committee would ask, "Who else is going to be on the committee?" "Who is going to talk to the city officials about our project?" "Who is going to promote the project to the church membership?" The concern is for the people involved and the interactions necessary. The melancholy will ask, "Do you have a set of plans?" "What is the budget and financial strategy?" "How about permits and construction bids, have you thought of everything?" For the melancholy, the devil and the Spirit is in the details. Finally, the phlegmatic on the building committee will say, "Tell me again, why do we need a new building?" The four personalities are like a checks and balance system, we need them all to function at our very best.

> *Old-book knowledge*: Now there are varieties of gifts, but the same Spirit; and there are varieties of service, but the same Lord; and there are varieties of activities, but it is the same God who empowers them all in everyone. (1 Cor. 12:4 –6, ESV)

Go with a Blueprint

- Learn about your temperament strengths and weaknesses.
- Learn about your spouse's temperament strengths and weaknesses.
- Don't use your weaknesses as an excuse for bad behavior.
- Use your strengths to improve your marriage.
- Accept your husband or wife for who they are: God's Creation!

Counselor Notes

The toughest personality combination in marriage is an off-the-charts, choleric wife, and an off-the-charts, phlegmatic husband. This is a tough combination because it can go against the grain of God's blueprint of marriage. The wife is naturally a leader and tends to not be submissive, especially if their husband is really laid back and not prone to take the leadership. Providing leadership does not mean that you have to be choleric, but you do have to take responsibility for channeling the choleric in a spiritually discerning way. In this case, the choleric wife must fight off the urge to usurp the husband's authority in the marriage, and the phlegmatic husband must force himself to take initiative when he feels more than willing to just let his wife handle it. It's key to remember in all personality conflicts that your relationship with Christ is the X factor. "But I say, walk by the Spirit, and you will not gratify the desires of the flesh." (Gal. 5:16, ESV).

Some other combination problems to be aware of in marriage are: sanguine and melancholy. Melancholies admire the sanguine's ability to relate easily to others, but sometimes, their messy, disorganized, and reckless ways do not work comfortably with compulsive, critical, and careful. Melancholies and phlegmatics can also have some pitfalls. The melancholy becomes impatient, and the phlegmatic feels personally attacked and put down. The melancholy feels unloved and unappreciated, and the phlegmatic feels humiliated and devalued. No personality issue has to be the end of a marriage, but understanding these challenges and approaching them in a loving and understanding way can prevent a world of unrest and discontent in your married life.

Not long ago, I worked with a melancholy-phlegmatic combination in counseling. Kyle, a small-business owner and loving father, was a neat and orderly and a very critical melancholy. His wife, Joanna, was a stay-at-home mom with the usual easy-going phlegmatic attitude toward life. Joanna felt demeaned and worthless and was ready to throw the marriage away. Kyle complained about everything that she did. Whatever she did, it was not good enough by Kyle's standards. One time, Kyle even got angry and went outside after coming home late from work to re-park the car because Joanna had parked it too many inches from the curb in front of their house. Kyle didn't really want a divorce, but Joanna didn't feel like she had it in her to continue.

After listening to their story, it became clear to me that they knew nothing about how to relate to each other. Kyle was being critical because he was wired to look at everything with an analytical mind. He didn't feel Joanna was worthless, he just wanted the best for her and the kids, but Joanna viewed his criticism as communicating a growing hatred toward her. Joanna's easygoing attitude and disinterest in doing things Kyle's way communicated a lack of appreciation and growing resentment toward him in Kyle's mind. Just taking a simple personality assessment and learning some basic skills about how to relate to each other in a new way turned their marriage around. They didn't look at everything as a personal attack, and they began to understand how to cope with each other's weaknesses and appreciate each other's strengths. Joanna found that doing certain things Kyle's way was easier and better for their household, saving money and time. Kyle found out that letting some little things go and enjoying a little disorganization once in a while made him feel closer to Joanna and the children. Kyle and Joanna still have their clashes, but a little understanding, with a pure motive, goes a long way. "Let us draw near with a true heart in full assurance of faith, with our hearts sprinkled clean from an evil conscience and our bodies washed with pure water." (Heb. 10:22, ESV).

Questions for Group Discussion

- What are some basic areas in your life that you and your spouse differ on?
- How is your natural temperament playing a role in your marital issues?
- In what ways do you and your spouse have different personas in public then at home?
- How will developing your character improve your marriage?
- What role does faith play in your personality struggles?

6

Elevation: The Love Platform

When it comes to marital discord, there seems to be three distinct periods in marriage where couples tend to fall into crisis and many go through divorce. The first period is the newlywed period, one to three years. In the newlywed period, many couples do not have the knowledge or skills necessary to negotiate this intense relationship and dissatisfaction grows rapidly. Often, without the concerns of children and deep financial ties, the option of divorce is a quick and easy solution, especially for those with little or no religious conviction. The second troubled period in marriage is the ten to fifteen-year mark. Here, the pressures of life, including raising children, negotiating careers, and dealing with financial ups and downs can be too much to cope with, and a couple can slowly and almost undetectably drift apart, become dissatisfied, and seek divorce, in hopes of a new start. The third distinct period is about the twenty-five-year mark or thereabouts. This is the so-called, "empty nest," stage of marriage. In this stage, couples that have drifted apart yet remained married must now focus on each other with less outside distraction from raising children and negotiating careers, etc. Unfortunately, life's pressures can still be very intense in this stage of life, dealing with aging parents and adult children along with the potential of added health concerns. A growing number of couples in this stage are seeking divorce as relief from emotional collapse in their relationship, past resentments, and disaffection.

In each of these troubled periods of marriage, we can see a direct link to the emotional health, or lack thereof, of the couple. Dr. Willard Harley in his book, *His Needs, Her Needs,*[12] points this out with his illustration of the love bank. The more emotional health, the greater the "love bank" balances. Increasing the deposits and reducing the withdrawals is key. I have used a similar concept for years in counseling and found it to be spot on. Our church has taught on emotional health in marriage with much success using, Dynamic Marriage, a class developed by Family Dynamics, incorporating Dr. Harley's books and research. I personally refer to the emotional health of partners in marriage as the Love Platform. Our love platform must be strong because it holds the weight of that mystical romantic love that we value so much in the marriage relationship. When the platform is weak, broken down, or gone, there is no love. A happy, healthy marriage requires a strong platform. So it only makes sense that we learn how to build this platform and then maintain it to keep a close, vital, and loving relationship.

The Platform Pillars

The platform itself has four supporting pillars: two female and two male. The pillars of safety and security are generally the female pillars, and they support all of her emotional health in marriage. She must feel safe and secure with her husband and their relationship in order to experience those feelings of love that these pillars uphold. When the husband says and does things that make her feel insecure or unsafe in some way, the loving feelings will tend to dissipate. The male pillars, on the other hand, tend to be honor and respect, all of the man's emotional health in marriage is wrapped up in the knowledge that he is honored and respected by his wife. His wife may be very loving and nurturing and caring, but if he feels un-honored or disrespected in any way, he will have a hard time with his own romantic feelings of love for her. For the woman, safety and security is often communicated through caring gestures, and for the man, honor and respect is often communicated through gestures of appreciation by the wife.

In the last several years, I have counseled many couples that are a lot like Ralph and Marie. Married for seven years with two small children, Ralph was a hard-working electrician, and Marie a stay-at-home mom who picked up extra cash for the family by running an unofficial daycare. Marie was becoming more and more insecure in the relationship because of Ralph's drinking habits. Ralph would work long hours with plenty of overtime, and he would unwind by having a few beers with the crew after the job. Without realizing it, he became extra aggressive, and his attitude in the home was different when he was drinking. As this pattern continued, Marie felt more and more unsafe in the relationship. Would Ralph be there when she needed him? Would his drinking become a problem? Would he eventually become abusive? What will happen with his relationship with the kids? These questions and more lingered in her mind and as her platform pillars weakened, she began to lose those loving feelings for Ralph.

This situation caused Marie's attitude to change, as she became more and more insecure, she became more and more nagging. "Why don't you stop drinking so much?" "Why don't you come home from work earlier?," "Why don't you spend more time with me and the kids?" she would complain. As far as Ralph was concerned, this nagging seemed a lot like disrespect. He would answer back, "I don't drink too much. I work hard and never miss. I bring home a good paycheck that you have no trouble spending on whatever you want." "I'm not four years old, so stop treating me like I am!" As Ralph's platform began to wobble, his feelings of love for Marie began to fade away.

This aspect of the "Love Platform" plays out over and over again. Emerson Eggerich in his book, *Love and Respect*[13] points out the craziness of this cycle in marriage. When the wife feels safe and secure; she has an easier time honoring and respecting her husband. When the husband feels honored and respected, he has an easier time loving his wife and providing safety and security in the relationship. When this safety and respect cycle gets out of whack, like the situations described with Ralph and Marie, someone has to, as my wife, Fran, says, "Man up!"

> *Old-book knowledge*: However, let each one of you love his wife as himself, and let the wife see that she respects her husband. (Eph. 5:33, ESV)

The Platform Building Blocks

These four pillars touch every aspect of our emotional health in marriage or our Love Platform and must be provided to our spouse by us in a healthy marriage. Let's look at some of these building blocks, the basis of which was first suggested by Dr. Harley and modified by me here to fit my understanding as demonstrated by the Love Platform.

- Relational Affection – Non-sexual touching, talking, and caring attitude (frequency, willingness, and initiative are important)
- Sex (frequency, willingness, and initiative are important)
- Caring Gestures – Genuine acts of lovingkindness (relationship in action)
- Friendship – Activities together (attitude and engagement is important)
- Trust – Honest and dependable (cornerstone of relationship)
- Appearance – Cleanliness and dress (making an effort, not looking for a ten)
- Financial Provision – Income (help in providing an acceptable standard of living)
- Household Support – Chores (help with the daily household tasks)
- Parenting – Present (engaged with the complete parenting process)
- Relational Contentment – Affirming and thankful (an attitude of delight in one's spouse)

These ten building blocks of your love platform are bonded together with what I have termed mortar elements, both male and female in nature. They include the more female elements of being cherished, feeling needed, and being known, participating in a giving relationship along with the more predominantly male elements of being admired, valued, and praised. That's not to say that men don't need to be cherished, needed, and known, and women don't need to be admired, valued, and praised, because these cementing blocks of marriage can be interchangeable for men and women in many cases.

Love Platform Building Blocks

Love Platform
Building Love Into Marriage

Romantic Feelings of Mysterious Love

Relational Affection

Sex

Cherished

Caring Gestures

Valued

Friendship

Praised

Trust

Admired

Appearance

Needed

Financial Provision

Household Support

Giving

Parenting: Engaged

Relational Contentment

Known

Secure and Safe

Honor and Respect

Relational Intimacy: Frequency, willingness and initiative are important

Sex: Frequency, willingness and initiative are important

Caring Gestures: Attitude & engagement are important

Friendship: Attitude and engagement are important

Trust: Usually requires over the top attention to details

Appearance: Important to both men and women but especially men

Financial Provision: In our society both men and women contribute but the ultimate responsibility, before God, is assigned to men

Household Support: Men are known for not doing their fair share but this can be a problem for women as well

Parenting: Spiritual formation and religious training are important

Relational Contentment: Affirming, thankful, joyful, appreciative and satisfied with your partner

In order to stay healthy and keep love flourishing in your marriage, you must maintain a healthy love platform. I usually recommend that couples identify their top five love platform building blocks. First, I tell them that they must pretend that each of these building blocks can reside in a vacuum and be separated from one another. Of course, in real life, they cannot be separated, and in many cases, you wouldn't want to have one without the other, but for the purposes of an exercise to rebuild or to strengthen your love platform, you must separate them out. Look at the ten building blocks and say, "My partner is only going to do one of these for me, which one do I want?" This now becomes number one on your list. Now do it again by saying, "Out of these nine left, my partner is only going to do one of these for me, which one do I want?" This now becomes number two on your list. After you have identified the top five, come together as a couple and reveal these to each other. Then explain specifically what it looks like to meet that need. In other words, if relational affection was your number one need, then you might say that means, "Giving me a hug every time you walk by, saying nice things to me several times a day, holding my hand when we walk in public, or look at me when we talk, etc." Finally, make a verbal commitment to each other to meet each other's top two needs, no matter what. It's good to know the top five, but I only want you to commit to the top two, because keeping the top two is going to kill you.

Finally, much attention must be given to the structure of your love platform. Like all structures, no matter how strong they are they must be inspected on a regular basis to guard against failures. Our emotional needs tend to change throughout our life, and so we must measure these things in our marriage from time to time. Obviously, a young, newlywed couple without children will not have parenting as a top emotional need, but as life progresses and children come along, our needs change as well, and if we don't identify this and make adjustments, our relationship could suffer from drifting and a weak love platform. A strong, healthy platform, coupled with spirit-filled living, is a recipe for success.

> *Old-book knowledge*: Woe to those who call evil good and good evil who put darkness for light and light for darkness, who put bitter for sweet and sweet for bitter! (Is. 5:20, ESV)

Get with a Blueprint

- Husbands, make your wife feel safe and secure with you in everything.
- Wives, make your husband feel honored and respected.
- Understand each other's top emotional needs in your relationship.
- Commit to meeting those needs.

- Build up each other's love platform, don't justify your bad behaviors.

Counselor Notes

Understanding the dynamics of the four pillars is the key to the love platform. It is almost as if God knew this when he had the apostle Paul write: "However, let each one of you love his wife as himself, and let the wife see that she respects her husband." (Eph. 5:33, ESV). Oh, yeah, that's right, remember, God knows more about you than you know about yourself. He is the creator and sustainer of all things. He's not saying that the husband shouldn't respect the wife or that the wife shouldn't love the husband, He's addressing our natural bents and laying us out a nice blueprint to having a loving, successful, God-honoring marriage. He even explains in the previous verses how love on the part of the husband is wrapped up in protecting, leading, and covering; in other words, safety and security. And the wife's respecting is tied to the attitude of honor as it is reflected in our own worship and fear of God—not just a positional respect, but a relational, earned respect.

All of the building blocks must be filtered through the understanding of these main support pillars as revealed to us by the scriptures.

1. Relational Affection: Not sexual in nature, includes talking, giving, acknowledging, expressing, touching. (Frequency, willingness and initiative are important.) Usually practiced and needed by women, more so than men. "Let love be genuine. Abhor what is evil; hold fast to what is good. Love one another with brotherly affection." (Rom. 12:9–10, ESV).

2. Sex: Usually a stronger desire for men (frequency, willingness, and initiative are important). "Do not deprive one another." (1 Cor. 7:5, ESV).

3. Caring Gestures: Attending to those little things, small acts of loving kindness (attitude and engagement are important) with

all humility and gentleness, with patience, bearing with one another in love. (Ephesians 4:2) "Likewise, husbands, live with your wives in an understanding way." (1 Pet. 3:7, ESV).

4. Friendship: Spending time with your spouse on hobbies and interests, the emphasis on activity, not on verbal interactions (attitude and engagement are important). "Do two walk together unless they have agreed to meet?" (Amos 3:3, ESV).

5. Trust: Complete honesty and dependability in their relationship (usually requires over-the-top attention to details) "Love...it does not rejoice at wrongdoing, but rejoices with the truth." (1 Cor. 13:6, ESV).

6. Appearance: Maintaining an appearance that is respectful of yourself and your spouse. (Important to both men and women, but it is especially important to men that their wives maintain appearance.) "Or do you not know that your body is a temple of the Holy Spirit within you, whom you have from God?" You are not your own. (1 Cor. 6:19, ESV). This does not mean that you or your wife must be super models, but it means there is an expectation that you will care for your body, which is the temple of the Holy Spirit in responsible ways. Men sometimes allow themselves to become unattractive to their wives by dressing sloppily, wearing clothes that don't match or are wrinkled, and not putting enough effort into the details of their appearance. Women can be notorious for dressing up and looking good for the public, but cracking out the sweats and ugly nightgowns for the husband's viewing pleasure.

7. Financial Provision: Providing a certain standard of living (in our society, both men and women contribute, but the ultimate responsibility before God is assigned to men). "But if anyone does not provide for his relatives, and especially for members of his household, he has denied the faith and is worse than an unbeliever." (1 Tim. 5:8, ESV). I have noticed a mild epidemic of men that are unwilling to sacrifice in any way to

provide for their wives and children. "Whoever is slack in his work is a brother to him who destroys." (Prov. 18:9, ESV).

8. Household Support: Helping with the daily needs of the household. (Men are known for not doing their fair share but this can be a problem for women as well.) "And whoever would be first among you must be slave of all." (Mk 10:44, ESV).

9. Parenting: Engaged in the raising and educating of your children (spiritual formation and religious training are important). "Train up a child in the way he should go; even when he is old he will not depart from it." (Prov. 22:6, ESV).

10. Appreciation: A real affirming attitude (not just appreciating what you do, but also who you are as a person) a thankful uplifting attitude toward your spouse. "Do nothing from selfish ambition or conceit, but in humility count others more significant than yourselves. Let each of you look not only to his own interests, but also to the interests of others." (Phil. 2:3–4, ESV).

These ten building blocks are not listed in any particular order of importance, with the exception of the first four. These first four are the key building blocks for our marriage relationship, especially in the first few years of marriage. Relational affection is generally very high on the woman's list of emotional needs. This aspect of relationship is nonsexual in nature, meaning we can have this kind of love with our kids and close friends and relatives, but as part of the love platform, it is exclusive to the marriage. This leads us to a problem in marriage right off the bat, since sex is commonly the number one emotional need of a man in the marriage relationship. There is a lot of relational affection displayed in sex, and the man may feel very affectionate toward his wife, while at the same time, failing to meet her true need of this non-sexual affection. Notice that I have termed both as relational. Sex was never intended by God to be apart from the committed marriage relationship. It is man that has separated it and made it something that it was never intended it to be.

God has always considered sex relational; when we make it just a physical act, we corrupt God's perfect design. An important note: I have discovered in about 25 percent of couples that I have worked with that these first two building blocks are reversed, with the woman having sexual intimacy higher on her list than the husband, but the same aspects of the platform hold true in reverse.

Secondly, we can immediately fall into problems with caring gestures and friendship in our marriage. Caring gestures are generally high on the woman's needs list, and friendship or companionship is generally high on the man's needs list. Men tend to be less impressed by the little caring things present in the marriage relationship and more physical, task, and solution–oriented, and women tend to be more aware of the little caring actions that are relationally oriented, but when the two meet each other in the middle, we have God's plan: a beautiful, creative design, that efficiently delivers practical results. When a woman says that she married her best friend, she means that she married somebody who is sensitive and does things that shows he cares. And when a man says that he married his best friend, he means that he has married somebody that he can hang out with and do things with.

I have found in my counseling sessions that getting these first four building blocks positioned correctly in marriage is essential to success in almost every other aspect of marriage and is quite often the underlying problem in most troubled, newlywed relationships. Consider these first four building blocks as chain rings, or the front sprockets on a bicycle, with relational affection and sex forming the large ring and caring gestures and friendship forming the smaller ring. The large ring provides power and stability, along with less pressure on the chain drive, and the smaller ring provides speed and ease with greater mobility in tougher uphill courses. Sex and relational affection as the main drive of the marriage provides stability and endurance, and will power you to where you need to go over great time and distances, and caring gestures and friendship are there to make the going easier when things get tough and the course seems more vertical. Caring gestures and friendship are useful in all kinds of diverse situations, but you could never travel long distances with such a small sprocket. It is only there to enhance the main sprocket of relational affection and sex, the oneness that drives the blueprint of God's design. The other building blocks of the platform are like rear driving sprockets, with trust probably being the largest, and the others varying from person to person. If you add sex to any relationship other than the marriage relationship, it will be like trying to travel a great distance using only small sprockets. This main sprocket was designed to be an exclusive driving force in marriage. Sex has always been God's design for making a great, enduring relationship between one man and one woman for life.

Sex Is Relationship

Relational affection and sex are designed to be one in the same. As previously stated, it is man (mankind) that has separated sex outside of relationship, not God. God has always intended that sex would be a key part of a committed relationship between a man and a woman.

God has made women more relational and men more physical in their drives, and neither one are broken. I believe that evil has corrupted sex and made it easy for us to separate it from God's intended purpose of relationship. Men are often encouraged, especially within the church, to put down their sexual natures and to be more relationally oriented toward their wives. Any man that concentrates too much on the sexual aspect of his relationship with his wife is considered worldly or unspiritual. Being relational without physical is a godly aspiration but, wait a minute, if God actually created sex to be part of that relationship, maybe this approach will not give us the blueprinted marriage that God has truly designed. When the wife, who is more relationally motivated, connects with her husband physically, she is practicing deliberate love, and when the husband, who is more physically motivated, connects with his wife relationally, he is practicing deliberate love, and this, I believe is God's true design.

Sex and relationship are received similarly by men and women. With sex, frequency is very important, especially to men. Often, the wife will feel more than adequate in her sexual frequency, but the husband has a habit of keeping track, and less is not more. For women, frequency is also important when it comes to relational affection; she is also keeping track and, for sure, more affection, attention, expressing, and giving is better than less. Willingness is also very important, attitude is everything. No husband wants to hear from his wife, "Let's get this over with!" when it comes to sex and when it comes to relational affection, no wife wants to hear her husband say, "What do you want to talk about now?" Initiative is also similar when it comes to sex versus relational affection. Women want to be pursued aggressively in relationship by their husbands, but since men are less relationally motivated, they seldom maintain an aggressive posture when it comes to relational affection with their wives. This is why women are drawn into affairs with men that show aggressive relational interest in them when their husband at home seems indifferent at best. And, likewise, the husband responds positively to the wife that shows initiative when it comes to their physical relationship. Women often suffer from poor self-esteem when it comes to their bodies; they understand that men are attracted to the female form, and that their husband must be looking for a more attractive body, thus, the interest in porn and other voyeuristic pleasures. The fact is that most men are not looking for the perfect ten. Not that they don't appreciate a ten, but they are usually more attracted to females that are aggressive sexually, thus the inappropriate interest in pornography, nude and topless bars, etc. It does as much for the husband when the wife shows initiative sexually as it does for the wife when the husband shows initiative relationally. When it comes to meeting these needs, we must look through the lens of the other. It's not our need, and if we don't look through our partner's filter, we'll miss the opportunity to provide emotional health and a platform for romantic love to exist in our marriage.

Trust: A Key Element

Trust is also a key building block in the Love Platform, and as stated, is also a large drive sprocket for pedaling through our life together. It's hard to maintain romantic feelings of mystical love with someone that you cannot trust. The Harts, in their book, *Safe Haven Marriage*,[14] show us the importance of being vulnerable with each other and having the kind of relationship that fosters secure attachment. This secure attachment with each other must grow out of a secure relationship with our Creator, who created us as relational beings. Then the Lord God said, "It is not good that the man should be alone; I will make him a helper fit for him." (Gen. 2:18, ESV). If we draw our strength, self-worth, and security from Jesus Christ, then we can afford to be vulnerable with each other. When we let each other down it is not the end of the world, we are whole and complete in Christ.

We guard our trust by being sexually pure. We do the most damage to our platform when trust is violated by sexual unfaithfulness. Usually, when an individual has trust rise to a high level on their love platform, it is because they have experienced some kind of infidelity with their current or past partner or some kind of breach of trust with one or both of their parents. The thing to remember when trying to deliberately meet this need is that it usually requires over-the-top attention. Often, those meeting this need in a spouse will say things like, "When will she trust me again?" "I call him every five minutes it seems!" or "Isn't this a bit much?" "How long do I have to keep doing this?" But what I say is, "What if it's forever?" "It most likely won't be, but what if it is?" Are you willing to show deliberate love and provide emotional health to your spouse in a way that fosters a loving and lasting relationship? Remember, it's not your need, look through the lens of your mate and understand how to sacrificially demonstrate the love of Christ as you attempt to restore trust to a broken or strained relationship.

Immediate Parenting

For many couples entering into second and third relationships, parenting can be a very important cog in the wheel. Oftentimes, people with children from a previous relationship draw a huge amount of emotional health from their new partner being a good parent to their kids. When the realities of blended family life set in, with pressures from biological parents, pressures from strained relationships, pressure from feeling the need to compete with a child for attention from your spouse, stepparents often fail to live up to their partner's expectations. Resentments begin to set in moreover, love is sucked right out of the relationship. The only solution is a godly solution we call adoption. When God receives us into His family an adoption takes place, we become joint heirs with Christ as legal sons of God. Even if a legal adoption is not possible, because both sets of biological parents are still available, a spiritual adoption in the mind of a stepparent must take place, and a trust in that adoption by their partner must also be recognized.

The parenting need can be a heavy emotional need, and if left unmet, can spell doom to your marriage. If you marry someone with children from another relationship, you will either become a great source of comfort and help, or a source of anxiety. You will make their life easier or more difficult, and usually nothing in between. It is like marrying somebody with a large student loan that must be repaid. When you marry them, it becomes your problem and your responsibility as well. If you resent them for having the loan, it will not change anything, but it will make you both more miserable. If you demand that the loan not be repaid because you have other uses for the money, it will ultimately come back to haunt you. Remember, one of God's overall purposes for marriage is the raising of godly children. Look at things from His perspective and adopt those children, at least in your mind, for His kingdom's sake.

Love Platform Complaints:

Complaint 1

I know when a couple doesn't really get it when they come back and say to me, "We tried this and it didn't work." It always works because the assignment is to provide emotional health to your spouse by deliberately loving them in meeting their needs by following Christ's example of sacrificial love. "For the love of Christ controls us, because we have concluded this: that one has died for all, therefore all have died; and he died for all, that those who live might no longer live for themselves but for him who for their sake died and was raised." (2 Cor. 5:14–15, ESV). We should be compelled to do this for each other because of what Christ did for us, but what they mean when they say that is, "I tried doing this, and I didn't get anything in return." The challenge is to meet your spouse's emotional needs whether or not they reciprocate in meeting yours. Of course, you have a better marriage when both are practicing deliberate love, but this does not negate your responsibility as an individual to honor God by sacrificially loving, even if your spouse does not return the favor.

Complaint 2

Another complaint that I often receive from couples whose love platform is seriously damaged or missing is that it feels somewhat mechanical to begin doing these things for each other. Compare this to practicing the spiritual disciplines in your relationship with Christ. Reading your Bible, praying, meditating, and going to church on Sunday at times may seem somewhat mechanical, but without these disciplines, you will not have a relationship with God and when you practice these disciplines on a regular basis, your relationship with God grows and blossoms into something that is anything but mechanical in nature. So it is with the love platform: these things must be practiced and become a regular part of your life, just like a spiritual discipline in order to have a loving, vibrant, and fulfilling marriage. Complaints aside, building a love platform works because it is the ultimate practice of deliberate Christian love in marriage.

Questions for Group Discussion

- How important is that mysterious romantic love to your marriage?
- How is a loss of passion playing a role in your marital issues?
- Do you think that some of the arguments and resentments you struggle with are from a broken down love platform? What building blocks need to be restored?
- How are the platform pillars playing a role in the dynamics of your marriage?

- How will re-building your platform change your marriage for the better? What is your part?
- What will prevent you from building your platform? What role does your faith play in it?

7

Plan Check: Love Inhibitors

When building, plan check reviews make sure that everything is up to code and ready to be built. It allows for adjustments to be made keeping everything updated to local building codes and requirements. There are some love inhibitors that need to be examined and put in plan check because of their ability to compromise the safety of your love platform and ruin the blueprint design.

To build and maintain a strong love platform is not enough. Now, you must identify some things in your marriage that attack your platform trying to chop down the supports from underneath it. Dr. Harley, in his book, *Love Busters*,[15] identifies some things that we do to bust or kill love in our marriage. Using his love bank analogy, we make deposits and withdrawals, and if you withdraw too much, you end up with a bounced check in the form of marital crisis. As long as you have gas in your car, you can drive around all day and not even give it a second thought, but as soon as the warning light comes on, you must begin driving with a plan that includes stopping at a gas station. If you run it down to empty, you will find yourself dead on the side of the road. In marriage, this is what oftentimes happens: we axe away at our love platform, never replacing or building up the supports. Eventually, the platform falls over and our marriage is like that car driven completely out of gas and stuck dead on the side of the road.

One summer, my wife, Fran, and I drove to Colorado for vacation. On the return trip home, I got a little overly focused on making time, and I buzzed right past the last gas stop in a very desolate part of Utah. Thirty plus miles beyond the last stop, and at least forty miles before the next highway stop, my gas light came on in the dashboard. The warning gave me a sinking feeling in my stomach. I told Fran that I had never run out of gas in my life, but the first time was going to be a doozy, out in the middle of nowhere without even cell phone service. My driving behavior changed immediately. My foot came off of the pedal and I slowed from seventy-five down to sixty miles per hour. I also turned off the air conditioning, even though it was over 100 degrees outside. We got lucky, and I exited the freeway to find a sparsely traveled path and a gas station that we were able to coast into on fumes. Of course, it was expensive, but the sky was the limit for keeping my car on the road at that point.

When it comes to your marriage, your behavior must change at the first sign of trouble as well. Of course, keeping your tank very full will prevent emergencies, but let's face it: you can't drive without running the tank down. When it comes to your love platform, there are behaviors that tend to chop at the pillars and chip away at the blocks. I call these love inhibitors. You're probably never going to eliminate them all together, but pulling your foot off the gas pedal and turning off the air conditioner will give you a fighting chance. Spend more time strengthening your platform than you do tearing it down.

> *Old-book knowledge*: "See that no one repays anyone evil for evil, but always seek to do good to one another." (1 Thess. 5:15, ESV)

Love Inhibitors

Unfortunately, I have discovered that today, many couples when faced with the reality that their marriage is dead on the side of the road, they just get out and walk away. I have talked to numerous individuals going through a divorce or in the aftermath of divorce, when questioned about preventative or interventional support received, reveal that no help or very little help was even sought. If it was their car, not their marriage, dead on the side of the road, they would make phone calls, walk distances, take time off work, and rearrange their schedules to make sure that their car was towed to a repair shop, and if they didn't have the money to pay for the repair, they would get out their credit card or do whatever it takes to facilitate the repair and get the car back on the road. But when it comes to marriage, sometimes a proportional amount of effort is not even made.

Since marital repairs are expensive, time-consuming, and many times nonexistent, we should take special care to prevent a sharp blade of an ax from chopping away at our platform. When our platform begins to fail, we begin to say things like, "I'm not so sure I even like her anymore," or "I'm pretty sure that I hate him." Once again, drawing from Dr. Harley's work, I have come to identify ten ax blades that I call Love Inhibitors. They are inhibitors because they are always present, in some form or another, inhibiting love in our marriage by chipping away at our emotional health.

Indignation: I'm Right, You're Wrong

Nothing good will come out of things you say in anger. Marriage needs to be a safe place for both of you to share and live together. Anger creates an unsafe environment. Win the argument or win your marriage. Another marriage will not just come along but another argument will.

Autonomy: Lone Ranger Mentality

Operating in a world of your own has its benefits, but a safe and loving marriage is not one of them. Autonomous behaviors without a safe connection (trust) may be the most dangerous of all tactics when it comes to negotiating a marriage. The blueprint calls for becoming one. This is not accomplished by an independent attitude. When two function as one, there needs to be not only close proximity, but harmonious action and intimate knowledge. This requires both people in the marriage to be aware and involved, at some level, in every aspect of each other's lives. Even the Lone Ranger had Tonto.

Critical Demeanor: You Need My Help

Criticism delivered wrongly creates withdrawal and triggers defensive responses. Do not confuse criticism with honesty. Criticism can be disguised as blatant honesty and be hurtful, not helpful. A well-meaning complaint states a problem but doesn't attack an individual's personhood. I've heard that all criticisms we receive, even from our enemies, has at least some element of truth to it. So it makes sense that if we took criticism better, we could benefit personally from it, but the fact remains that we don't take criticism too well, even when it is constructive. In fact, you generally will spend less time with and not be drawn to people that tend to criticize you. So, this being the case, it is a bad idea to nurture a critical demeanor with your husband or wife. It will not only inhibit love, but chop away at your platform, making your marriage weak in other areas as well. We all have our critics to contend with; we don't need our spouse to be one of them.

Defensive Posture: Oh No, You Don't!

Most defensive attitudes come from an unwelcome criticism, so you must begin to understand your part in the process and begin to let go of those self-protective responses. As stated before, almost all criticisms have at least a small element of truth to them, and listening to them with a soft heart allows you to be vulnerable with your partner, and in turn, creates a secure place to live and love. Once we enter into a defensive posture, there is no communication or connection that can take place. Therefore, we must risk being hurt in order to have closeness with our valued partner.

Deception: Lies and More

We naturally are not attracted to those who lie to us. Lying to someone is like not valuing them as an equal or trusting them as a partner or respecting them as a leader. Once you find out that someone in your normal circle lies to you, the relationship changes. We not only distrust liars, but we tend to avoid them, and it is hard to avoid someone that you are married to. A safe marriage is one that is open and honest in both the big and little areas of life. Practicing deception goes beyond lying; it can be withholding information or feelings. Practicing deception in any form will create that giant vacuum-sucking sound of love leaving your marriage as quick as a blink of the eye. Nothing can destroy your spirit faster than to find out the most important person in your life has deceived you.

Disrespect: You Just Don't Get It

This is often the number one love killer for men in the relationship. The problem is not disagreeing on certain issues, but not respecting each other, which is often the culprit to lost love in marriage. Author, Shaunti Feldhahn, based on research for her book, *For Women Only*, discovered, "Three out of four men indicated that if they had to choose between feeling inadequate and disrespected by everyone, or alone and unloved, they would choose feeling alone and unloved."[16] Though it may be more acute in men over women, disrespect is a sharp axe to the platform in your marriage, whether male or female. You shouldn't be afraid to disagree, but you should be very cautious to not be disrespectful.

Irritating: Good and Bad Habits

Avoid behaviors that irritate your spouse. Good and bad, as far as habits go, may be in the eye of the practitioner. Pride should not stand in the way of our love and concern for another, particularly our spouse. Little irritating behaviors do not define our personhood and can be easily given up to show love and concern. Otherwise, irritations can build and become interpreted as thoughtlessness, inconsiderate, and unkind behavior. This may not be the sharpest axe in the tool shed when it comes to tearing away at your platform, but it may be the final blow or the straw the breaks the camel's back as we say.

When Fran and I were newlyweds, I had the habit of drinking milk right from the carton. I would go straight to the fridge and open the door and grab and drink. This annoyed Fran to no end, even though it was no big deal to me. Eventually, I realized that it was inconsiderate and showed a lack of concern for her feelings as I continued to do it my way. So I began to change my habit, and I would force myself to get a glass from the cupboard before going to the fridge. It was difficult at first, and an inconvenience, as far as I was concerned, but it helped our love platform stay strong, so ultimately it was worth the effort. Avoiding the irritation of your spouse for an insignificant reason is one of the easiest fixes in marriage, so what does it say about you if you're not willing to make the effort? Now after thirty-nine years of marriage, I can't even force myself to drink out of the carton. I find myself going for a glass even when Fran is not around, and the funny thing is that now it irritates me if I see someone else drinking from the carton, go figure.

Indifference: Hello, Is Anybody Home?

In most cases, an attitude of indifference is more hurtful to us then outright rejection. It subtly tells us that we are not even worthy of emotion. I have seen a number of marriages continue on for decades when both the husband and the wife were indifferent, but when one spouse is indifferent and the other is not, it leads to resentment and overwhelming contempt by the offended spouse. Indifference on the part of a single spouse will almost universally end the marriage. When *indifference* becomes the best word to describe our marriage, we act as though we are dead to each other, and there are often feelings of numbness and a lack of response to each other's presence.

Bitterness: I Can Never Forgive You

A safe marriage that maintains closeness and a sense of security is a place where two people realize their need to forgive and to seek forgiveness. Resentfulness develops when we hang on tightly to areas where we feel we have been wronged, and we allow ourselves to become bitter. Bitterness, like indifference, often leads to divorce.

Selfishness: It's For Your Own Good

"When Mama is happy, everyone is happy." "If you would just keep me happy, life would be sweet," familiar phrases with a selfish tone. A selfish attitude or desire leads us into making unfair requests of our spouse, but we usually don't perceive such requests as selfish or unfair, we just fail to fully understand the perspective of our spouse when it differs from our own. It is more common for us to take the time to understand the perspectives of people outside of our marriage than it is for us to understand the perspectives of our spouse. We know what is good for them, if they'd only listen.

Go With a Blueprint

- Rate each other on these Love Inhibitors. Use a 1–10 Scale with 1 representing no problem and 10 representing a severe problem in your marriage.
- Commit to reducing your behaviors that inhibit love in your marriage.

Counselor Notes

This side of heaven, warring in our flesh, we will never be able to completely eliminate these love inhibitors in our relationships, but we can reduce their effects as we strive to live a life worthy of our high calling in Christ Jesus. His divine power has granted to us all things that pertain to life and godliness, through the knowledge of him who called us to his own glory and excellence (2 Peter 1:3).

Indignation

Self-righteous anger, or anger in and of itself, is not a sin. It is a God-given emotion, but we have come to associate that emotion directly with sin because of the actions it produces in our angry moments. Indignation is particularly harmful in marriage because you've directed judgment against your spouse leading to anger.

Righteous indignation tends to have a negative angle to it because we inherently understand that we are not more righteous than anyone else, even if we feel like we are in any given situation, thus the term *self-righteous*. "Know this, my beloved brothers: let every person be quick to hear, slow to speak, slow to anger; for the anger of man does not produce the righteousness of God." (Jas 1:19–20, ESV).

Autonomy

I counseled with a couple that had been drifting apart in what was otherwise a pretty good marriage, when I found out that each had aspects of their lives that the other knew nothing about. What I learned from them is this: if your husband plays in an adult baseball league, you don't have to go to every game or be the scorekeeper or water girl, but you better know everything important about that team. For instance, what challenges does your husband face on the team? What is the toughest team in the league to beat? You get the picture. Often, we are involved at this level before marriage when we were dating or are with kids and their activities, but when it comes to our involvement with each other in certain areas after marriage, we are clueless. An unwritten expectation in marriage is that you care about this person more than any other person on the planet, meaning you will know baseball even if you don't know baseball, if baseball is part of your partner. "Walk in a manner worthy of the calling to which you have been called, with all humility and gentleness, with patience, bearing with one another in love, eager to maintain the unity of the Spirit in the bond of peace." (Eph. 4:1–3, ESV).

Critical Demeanor

"Too many people have the gift of critiquing and not enough people have the gift of encouraging. Do all things without grumbling or disputing." (Phil. 2:14, ESV).

Defensive Posture

"Let God be your shield and defender. A soft answer turns away wrath but a harsh word stirs up anger." (Prov. 15:1, ESV).

Deception

Satan lied to Eve because he did not value her as a person. Satan, the father of lies, will always tell you what you want to hear, "Sure, go ahead and eat that fruit, you won't really die." "If you eat that fruit, you will be like God." Satan didn't care if Eve walked over the cliff to her death because he didn't value her. That crafty serpent didn't care if Eve had misinformation because it would lead to her death, not to her well-being, and that was his ultimate agenda with her. God never lies to us even about the hard truths because he does value us. He doesn't want us to be misinformed because he wants to prevent harm from coming to us. "A gentle tongue is a tree of life, but perverseness in it breaks the spirit." (Prov. 15:4, ESV).

Disrespect

"Respecting each other is a way to mirror our relationship with God as we honor His wants and desires in our life. Honor everyone. Love the brotherhood. Fear God. Honor the emperor." (1 Pet. 2:17, ESV).

Irritating

"Remember eliminating irritations is the easiest way to show love. Love one another with brotherly affection. Outdo one another in showing honor." (Rom. 12:10, ESV).

Indifference

This is the ultimate expression of "I don't care." Indifference is not only offensive to us in our relationship with each other, it is offensive to God in our relationship with Him. God hates our indifference because he wants our hearts, and when somebody has your heart, it is impossible to remain indifferent to anything they say or do. "I know your works: you are neither cold nor hot. Would that you were either cold or hot! So, because you are lukewarm, and neither hot nor cold, I will spit you out of my mouth. (Rev. 3:15–16, ESV) "And we desire each one of you to show the same earnestness to have the full assurance of hope until the end, so that you may not be sluggish, but imitators of those who through faith and patience inherit the promises." (Heb. 6:11–12, ESV). No indifference here!

Bitterness

Bitterness is a spiritual problem, and it will trump love in our marriage every time. Christ takes a dim view of an unforgiving attitude in light of the forgiveness that he has given to us. I have recently added forgiveness to the traditional vows in my own personal ceremony that I use when officiating a wedding. I make both the bride and groom vow to extend forgiveness when they have been wronged and to seek forgiveness when they have done wrong. I have come to understand that we must not only be willing to forgive and seek forgiveness in marriage, but we must make a vow before God and man to seek and extend forgiveness in marriage. It is necessary because marriage cannot exist without it, and bitterness is the byproduct of an unforgiving spirit. Our relationship with God requires us to seek forgiveness if it is to remain stable. Our marriage relationship, which represents our relationship with God, is no different; forgiveness must be an active value in our marriage if it is to continue.

In the parable of the wicked servant, the king forgives the servant of a debt he could not repay, 10,000 talents, or the equivalent of about 200,000 years of wages at the time. The servant in turn goes and attempts to cruelly collect about four month's pay from his servant, and throws him in debtor's prison when he cannot pay. When the king finds out, he is angry and rescinds his former grace to the wicked servant. The parable teaches us that God has forgiven us of a debt we cannot repay. Through the blood of His Son, Jesus Christ, we no longer have to suffer the worst fate that a man can face, a type of debtor's prison. Since God has forgiven us such an enormous debt, from His perspective, there is no debt that we cannot forgive someone else, as He extends his grace to us, He expects us to do the same, even in marriage. "Then Peter came up and said to him, 'Lord, how often will my brother sin against me, and I forgive him? As many as seven times?' Jesus said to him, 'I do not say to you seven times, but seventy-seven times.'" (Matt. 18:21–22, ESV).

Selfishness

Treating others better than ourselves is a decidedly biblical principle and cannot be ignored in marriage. Your marriage is a good barometer for your spiritual condition. If you can't exercise the fruits of the Spirit in your marriage, then it doesn't matter how well you do at church or in public, you're just putting on a façade. "Man looks on the outside, but God looks at the heart." The way you live out your marriage is a reflection of your true heart. "Do nothing from selfish ambition or conceit, but in humility count others more significant than yourselves. Let each of you look not only to his own interests, but also to the interests of others." (Phil. 2:3–4, ESV).

Because we war not against flesh and blood but against principalities and powers, it will be all but impossible for these inhibitors or axe blades that attack your love platform to be completely eliminated. Reducing the effects of these love inhibitors will make it easier for you to maintain a strong platform by providing emotional health for your spouse. Returning to the car analogy used earlier, the emotional health provided in the love platform is the fuel that powers the car, and the love inhibitors are the accelerators that burn the fuel as the car travels down the road. As long as you're putting in more fuel than you're taking out, you'll be able to stay on the road. Burning fuel more efficiently makes it easier to keep the tank full. So when it comes to your marriage, you need to drive a hybrid. "For we do not wrestle against flesh and blood, but against the rulers, against the authorities, against the cosmic powers over this present darkness, against the spiritual forces of evil in the heavenly places. Therefore take up the whole armor of

God that you may be able to withstand in the evil day, and having done all, to stand firm." (Eph. 6:12–13, ESV).

Questions for Group Discussion

- On the 1–10 scale, what key inhibitors of yours are negatively affecting your spouse?
- What is your inner voice telling you about correcting some of your behaviors?
- How would your spouse respond if you did change some of your negative behaviors?
- Can you think of some other reasons besides your marriage for changing your behaviors?
- Describe your personal spiritual battle in marriage.
- Is this a battle that we can win? How do we fight it?

8

Systems: The "DARE" Marriage

When my wife, Fran, and I did our premarital counseling about thirty-nine years ago, we met in a little trailer in the backyard of my baseball coach's backyard. He was not only my baseball coach, but our Bible teacher from school. My wife and I attended a Christian high school back in the day. We met and became friends when she volunteered to be the scorekeeper on my high school baseball team. Since we were only eighteen years old when we got married, my coach, who was also a Bible teacher, was the obvious choice in my mind to marry us. Of course, my parents thought our pastor would be a better choice, so we compromised and had both do our ceremony. I eventually performed my youngest son's wedding, but in a foreseeable, like-father-like-son fashion, my two older boys chose to be married by their high school football coach, Dan Finfrock.

Anyway, our pastor made it legal, but my high school baseball coach did our premarital counseling. We met a couple of times and went through a little book by Norman Wright, called *Communication the Key to Marriage*.[17] Looking back, my coach did the best he could, but that was the extent of our counseling. To his credit, that was a very good book by a respected author that is still used by many today. Communication is a key aspect of marriage, and I don't want to just breeze over the topic because it sounds too familiar. It is relevant today. I have more than a few couples that come into my office and tell me first thing that they have a failure to communicate. Good communication will not solve all of your marital discord, but it is a sure bet that nothing will be solved without it.

As for the blueprint, blueprints usually detail many different systems within a building: electrical, plumbing, heating, and air conditioning, etc. Likewise, communication drives all of the systems in our marriage, but before we discuss how to communicate, let's set some ground rules for what not to do when it comes to communicating with your spouse. Pastor Tommy Nelson of the Song of Solomon Marriage Conferences [18] has a list, "17 Nevers of Communication with Your Spouse." Here is his list that my wife and I obtained at his marriage conference a number of years ago:

- Never raise your voice in your home
- Never publicly embarrass your mate
- Never argue in front of the kids
- Never use the kids to win an argument
- Never talk negatively about your spouse outside of your marriage
- Never use sex to win
- Never touch in anger
- Never call names
- Never get historical and take into account a wrong suffered
- Never stomp out
- Never freeze out your mate
- Never use the in-laws
- Never reason in the face of pain
- Never let the sun go down on your anger
- Never reverse an argument
- Never fail to listen to your mate
- Never harden yourself toward your spouse

Negative Talk

I would like to focus in on one that made a profound difference in my own marriage. Never talk negatively about your spouse outside of your marriage. Talking negatively will breed seeds of discontent in your marriage, and it also becomes a form of self-fulfilling prophecy in our lives as well. I don't know how Fran and I figured this out at such a young age, but from the very start, we made a vow not to talk about each other behind our backs. We must have heard a pastor or teacher somewhere talk about this, but as far as I know, neither one of us has ever violated this vow, and of all the things that have contributed a positive impact on our marriage, this ranks near the top.

Do you know how freeing it is to have a relationship where your spouse is your number one protector when it comes to your reputation? Even when my wife would be well within her rights to badmouth me to others, she chooses to love me by not venting. This is real love. One thing I have observed guys doing over the years is standing around at work and venting on their wives. She won't let me do this or that and she tells me this or that and she complains or spends too much money or doesn't fix dinner, ruins the car, or spoils the kids, etc. You know what I mean, we are just venting when we say things like that, but it ruins our spouse's reputation. I knew some guys at my previous job that vented on their wives quite a bit. I understood that they didn't set out to damage their wife's reputation with me, but they did. I understood the dynamics, but when my wife and I would be out to dinner or some event with them and their wives, I couldn't help but think what a bad, unpleasant wife she must be, and when something bad would happen between them, instead of trying to help, I would catch myself saying, "Well, of course this happened because that is just the way that she is." The husband's venting became self-fulfilling prophecy in their marriage, and I, like others, interjected bad sentiment into their marriage because we had been trained to do so by all the negative talk.

Fran and I worked with a young woman a few years ago that violated this principle we had taught her. She decided to take an opportunity to vent on her husband to some female friends. Of course, he eventually found out about it through their husbands, and the next thing you know, we end up at their house, trying to help them sort things out. I asked her if venting to her friends made her feel better and she said, "Yes, it did." I asked, "How long did that last?" She said, "A few minutes." I asked, "How long have you and your husband been fighting over this?" She said, "Weeks." Was it worth it? She admitted, "Probably not." Venting does make us feel better, this is one of the benefits of counseling and the general rule is: You should never talk negatively about your spouse to anyone who is not in a position to help your marriage, and your friends and relatives and those in your normal circle of relationships are not in a position to help your marriage. Seek out a counselor or a mentor or a pastor or someone that is in a position to help your marriage and will not be easily biased by the circumstances of your current situation. This young couple found out the hard way the benefit of keeping this general rule. There's a difference between being real and honestly sharing your struggles as a couple with friends and relatives versus venting and speaking negatively about each other to those same friends and relatives. Speaking negatively will only bring negativity back into your marriage from outside sources, and speaking positively will bring positive influence into your marriage from outside sources. Fran and I have always had our marriage upheld by our friends and peers as a good one, and one to look upon as an example and help to others. Does this mean that we have a perfect marriage without difficulty? No, but it does mean that we have a marriage with a positive outlook and hope for the future, with our positive outlook being reflected back to us by our friends, family, and peers.

I once had a young lady disagree with me vehemently about this view. She claimed that she and her mother had such a close relationship that she felt comfortable sharing every detail with her, even the negatives about her husband. The only thing that I can tell you if you have the same view as this young lady is what I told her that day, "Write this day down, mark the date on your calendar. I don't know when and I don't know exactly why, but someday, you'll look back on this conversation and say, 'Gary was right.'" I am that confident that talking negatively about your spouse will come back and bite you. There are already enough people in the world that will be happy to talk negatively about your spouse; you don't need to be one of them.

Negative Talk and Children

This principle should also hold true with your children. A few years ago, one of my daughter-in-laws came to me and wanted to discuss some negatives about their marriage. She became somewhat frustrated as I failed to engage her in a way that would help her vent her feelings. She said, "Well, you and Fran never had these kinds of problems." I said, "How would you know?" She said, "Your son told me that you never had these problems." I said, "Let me tell you something, Fran and I have had all of these problems, and some that you have not even thought of yet, but our son was not privy to that information." You see, your children are not in a position to help your marriage, so why should you be talking negatively about each other to your children? Even your children will speak positive or negative influences back into your marriage, and you will be influencing and shaping their ideas of marriage in a negative way. Spend your time looking for and promoting the good in your spouse, not the negative.

> *Old-book knowledge*: Finally, brothers, whatever is true, whatever is honorable, whatever is just, whatever is pure, whatever is lovely, whatever is commendable, if there is any excellence, if there is anything worthy of praise, think about these things. (Phil. 4:8, ESV)

"D A R E" Marriage

Once you understand that there is a proper time and place and person that you should talk to about your marriage issues, you should also understand that one place you should be able to speak truth, both positive and negative, is with each other. Having a marriage where safe communication can take place is what I call a D A R E marriage. A D A R E marriage will show acts of deliberate love, it will demonstrate hearts that are accessible, it will reveal responsive spirits, and it will demonstrate an engaged way of living and processing information together. Sue Johnson, in her book, *Hold Me Tight: Seven Conversations for a Lifetime of Love,*[19] introduces the A R E conversation, as a way of better understanding each other, controlling negative reactions, and developing a secure bond in your marriage relationship. I have added the value of deliberate love as a starting point to this kind of communication. Adding this one element to the process guarantees success in situations where many fail.

Deliberate Love

Love is a decision. It's not uncommon to hear professionals these days talk about the natural course of marriage and how the passion fades. Loss of passion is an inevitable part of marriage and relationship. The Clarks, in their book, *Passion that Lasts a Lifetime*,[20] explain how to have a lifetime of passion. We should never settle for a marriage that lacks passion, but unlike what we've been taught by romance novels and movies, it is not something that happens mysteriously out of our control, we must pursue it diligently and deliberately. It is something that we must make happen not watch happen. Deliberate love is the ultimate form of self-awareness, and a good beginning point for all meaningful conversation.

Accessibility

Many of us have encountered an inaccessible boss in our workplaces. This is the boss that doesn't know what your problems and concerns are and is just as happy to keep it that way. They usually have a "my way or the highway" mentality, and they don't leave you feeling very warm and fuzzy at all. On the other hand, we all love the boss that has an open-door policy, and is willing to let you vent and talk out all of your concerns and issues. This approach makes us feel appreciated and valuable. In marriage, being accessible to each other for these types of communications is very important to feeling appreciated and cared for as well. Have an open-door policy with your spouse.

Responsiveness

Okay, an open-door policy without responsiveness is almost worse than a closed-door policy. You know what I mean. Many of us have also experienced the boss with the open-door policy that smiles and listens to all of your concerns and then immediately forgets you even had a conversation. The moment you walked out that open door, it was as if you never came in. This leaves you feeling empty and used. It gets your hopes up, and then lets you come crashing down. Don't just leave a door open for your spouse, but respond with action to their concerns when they come through that door. Example: "We don't ever have time for romance anymore." Response: "Let's go out for a quiet romantic dinner next Friday."

Be Engaged with Your Spouse

Attitude is everything. I know when I am really valued as an employee when my boss leaves his door open and responds to my concerns with action, but I feel part of team when he follows up and engages with me in a concerned, ongoing way. Your spouse wants to know that you're with them. Example: "Maybe we need to go out for a romantic dinner every month to keep the fire burning? What do you think?" Now, you're not only responding to their concerns, but you're fully engaged with them in the ongoing process of relationship. You care because love is deliberate and engaged!

> *Old-book knowledge*: Love is patient and kind; love does not envy or boast; it is not arrogant or rude. It does not insist on its own way; it is not irritable or resentful; it does not rejoice at wrongdoing, but rejoices with the truth. Love bears all things, believes all things, hopes all things, endures all things. (1 Cor. 13:4–7, ESV)

Go with a Blueprint

- Never talk negatively about your spouse with anyone that is not in a position to help your marriage.
- Practice deliberate love in your relationship.
- Have an open-door policy with your husband or wife
- Respond to your spouse's concerns with action.
- Engage your husband or wife with an ongoing caring attitude.

Counselor Notes

Deliberate Love

I have added the biblical value of deliberate love to demonstrate our responsibility to God in this process. This one element guarantees success when our normal human motivations fail us. For this is a gracious thing, when, mindful of God, one endures sorrows while suffering unjustly. For what credit is it if, when you sin and are beaten for it, you endure? But if when you do good and suffer for it, you endure, this is a gracious thing in the sight of God. For to this you have been called, because Christ also suffered for you, leaving you an example, so that you might follow in his steps. (1 Pet. 2:19–21, ESV). In other words, we are called to a higher standard of living, the sacrificial love of Christ. If we apply this verse to marriage what it is saying is: if you are a lousy husband or wife and your spouse returns the favor, so what, you're getting what you deserve. But if you sacrificially love your husband or wife for the sake of obedience to Christ, and suffer for it because your spouse does not return the favor, this is commendable before God. In this case, God stands up and takes notice of your actions. You receive an accommodation, and He guarantees that your actions will not go unrewarded. We are called to deliberate love in marriage and proper communication is one form of deliberate love that we can exercise in a godly fashion.

Accessible Heart

Accessibility can leave us vulnerable to each other, but we can be vulnerable because the Lord is our strength in times of weakness and trouble. When our strength comes from the Lord, we are more capable of being vulnerable with each other, but when our strength comes from the accessibility and responsiveness of our spouse, we tend to be more guarded because failure and rejection are more devastating to our well-being. "Likewise, husbands, live with your wives in an understanding way, showing honor to the woman as the weaker vessel, since they are heirs with you of the grace of life, so that your prayers may not be hindered." (1 Pet. 3:7, ESV). When we make ourselves inaccessible to our spouse, God makes Himself inaccessible to us.

Responsive Spirit

> And when Jesus came to the place, he looked up and said to him, "Zacchaeus, hurry and come down, for I must stay at your house today."
>
> For the Son of Man came to seek and to save the lost.
>
> (Lk 19:5, 10, ESV)

Jesus not only made himself accessible to Zacchaeus when he needed Him, but he responded to his inner need of relationship and salvation. In spite of his reputation with the Jews, Jesus responded to Zacchaeus's reaching out to Him. Accessibility is just the beginning. What would have been accomplished if Jesus had just stopped and talked to Zacchaeus up in that tree and then moved on without responding to his real need? Do you listen to your husband or wife sometimes, without really trying to understand and respond to the deeper need that is trying to be communicated? Are you fond of the boss with the open-door policy that immediately dismisses your concerns when you leave the room? Accessibility is important in a relationship, but responsiveness is needed for a deeper level of connection and trust.

Engaged Living

"But if we walk in the light, as he is in the light, we have fellowship with one another, and the blood of Jesus his Son cleanses us from all sin." (1 Jn 1:7, ESV). Notice how walking in relationship with God is accomplished by walking in the light together with His Son. Engaged living is buying into the process and walking together through it. Engagement should come across as enthusiasm for your spouse's well-being as you walk through life's ups and downs together. "Look down from heaven and see, from your holy and beautiful habitation. Where are your zeal and your might? The stirring of your inner parts and your compassion are held back from me." (Is. 63:15, ESV). Here Isaiah describes engaged living as he seeks it from God. Communicate with your spouse using all of your zeal and talent to engage, remembering that your spouse is not a problem to be dealt with but a potential problem solver to relate with.

Questions for Group Discussion

- How is going negative on your spouse affecting your marriage?
- How would it feel to have your spouse as your number one promoter as opposed to your number one critic?
- How do others in your circle of family, friends, and peers view your marriage?
- How has negative talk affected your viewpoint of other marriages around you?
- What prevents you from having an open-door policy with your spouse?
- In what ways do you respond to your spouse's concerns with action? In what ways does your spouse respond to your concerns with action?
- In your mind, how important is your spouse's attitude in the communication process?

9

Sectional View: The Spoon Method

Generally, a single-dimensional view of an object or layout in a blueprint is inadequate in giving a complete perspective. Varied views can give a more precise perspective of the drawing detail and pulling out a section of the drawing allows for clearer and finer detail. Good communication works this way in marriage as it gives us greater perspective and understanding of what we're trying to build, where we are at in the process, and how we are going to get where we want to go.

Many years ago, my wife Fran and I were trained as marriage mentors by Pastor Kent Dyer and his wife from First Baptist Church in Pomona, California. He taught us and several other couples a communication technique he referred to as "The Spoon Method." I have since come to realize that the spoon method is not only a learning tool that helps us to listen and speak more effectively within marriage, but it is also the mechanics of a good "D A R E" marriage conversation. Fran and I have successfully taught this method to hundreds of couples. Our version doesn't look much like the original we learned many years ago, but we have thoroughly enjoyed watching many of the pre-married and married couples decorate their wooden or plastic spoons as a memory keepsake as they learn how to create more intimacy and friendship in their communication style.

The Spoon Method: Deliberate Love

Practicing the spoon method itself is an act of deliberate love in marriage. The spoon method is designed to help us do a better job of actively listening and effectively speaking to one another. In the spoon method, one partner gets the spoon out when they need to have a serious conversation, setting the spoon in an obvious place for the partner to see. At this point, an act of deliberate love has already been demonstrated because the individual invoking the spoon conversation has already put aside their emotions and calmed down, waiting for a more productive time to engage their spouse. This is a form of self-awareness to understand your own personal flooding of emotion, and give way to a more godly influence before reacting inappropriately and unkind in speech and action.

The spoon being set out can be the trigger for both partners to check their defensive attitudes and approach one another in a spirit of love and concern. The spouse that first gets out the spoon will hold the spoon first when both agree it is time to talk. The person without the spoon is considered the helper. The job of the helper is to patiently listen and fully understand. Only the individual holding the spoon can speak, and only when the spoon is passed to the helper may the helper respond. The speaker becomes the helper, and the helper with the spoon now becomes the speaker.

When we try to communicate, especially in emotionally charged situations, without the spoon method, we tend to become defensive, angry, and argumentative. We are not really listening or understanding our partner's point of view. We begin talking over one another, answering and responding before the issue has been fully communicated, and we often times introduce concepts that are foreign and historically irrelevant to the issue at hand. When calming does occur, there is rarely complete resolution and misunderstandings are carried forward, providing fuel for future misunderstandings and a repeated cycle of anger, confusion, and disconnection. Therefore, deliberate love becomes the means by which we can begin to foster effective communication in our relationship.

> *Old-book knowledge*: A hot-tempered man stirs up strife, but he who is slow to anger quiets contention. (Prov. 15:18, ESV)

The Spoon Method: Listen and Speak Better

Accessibility in the spoon method means that both the speaker and the helper are available and willing participants. The helper must close off their feelings and strive to not be defensive. The helper must relinquish control and allow the speaker to be the authority on their own feelings and thoughts, and the helper must focus attention on the speaker alone, summarizing their thoughts, and asking questions in order to gain a clearer understanding of what is trying to be communicated. This is a proper response to your partner in establishing safe communication. You can always tell when the helper has become defensive or just isn't willing to listen when the first thing they do, when it's their turn to speak with the spoon, is to jump right into their own counterpoints and thoughts. When somebody really wants to understand and get it right, the first thing they must do is ask questions and clarify facts. When both buy into this process: deliberate love, accessibility, responsiveness, and engaged living can occur. Unresolved hurts and past negative outcomes will be a hindrance to this process. Developing the "D A R E" marriage, as spoken of already, is the goal. The spoon method, if allowed, is also a good way to explore past hurts and negative outcomes and provide a dais for forgiveness and acceptance.

The spoon may seem like a puerile little prop, but it can be an effective tool in promoting active listening and effective speaking. Fran and I have seen many couples improve their communication and relational awareness by demonstrating to them the spoon method and making them decorate their plastic and wooden spoons as little marital keepsakes and a present reminder of how they should be communicating and listening to one another in an active way. In active listening, you listen for the meaning of the words your partner is using and not just the words alone. The spoon method trains us to avoid interruptions and allows us to listen better and take better mental notes of what is going on. It encourages feedback and questioning and allows a great deal of concentration to be focused on your spouse while communicating. Effective speaking is accomplished by revealing your feelings while not putting your partner on the defensive. If you can picture yourself pointing your finger at your partner while you are speaking, you are not being and effective speaker. As you speak, you should be pointing the finger at yourself. Example, "I am feeling a little unloved today" vs. "You are not showing me love today." Notice which way your finger is pointing in these statements. Utilizing the spoon method in your communication is just a loving way to build a closer relationship through conversation.

Old-book knowledge: A soft answer turns away wrath, but a harsh word stirs up anger. (Prov. 15:1, ESV)

Listening Is Love

Listening to one another is one of the greatest ways to show love. We are not attracted to people who do not listen to us, in addition, we generally avoid spending time with them. In fact, the very core of who we are as individuals is influenced by how we perceive others are listening to us at the deepest level. Let me give you a personal example of how someone listening, or failing to listen, affects our self-esteem, and ultimately, our social interactions and attitudes. On one occasion, I was listening to a prominent pastor speak at a meeting. After the meeting, I had the opportunity to speak one to one with this pastor. The post meeting area was a little chaotic, and in the middle of our conversation, he was distracted and began speaking with somebody else. I thought to myself, *Wow, what am I chopped liver?* But I got over it pretty quickly because of the circumstances. On a different occasion, I had an opportunity to speak with the same pastor again. This time, the circumstances were not quite as hectic, but the exact same thing happened—he became distracted and pulled away from me in the middle of our conversation. This time, I was not quite so forgiving, and I stiffened and welled up with indignation. I said in my mind, *oh, this guy has nothing to say to me. I don't care how great a man of God he is, he's got nothing to say to me. I'm done with him.* Of course, I eventually got over it and realized that he did still have something to say to me, we were never going to be best friends, but God could still use him in my life because I was able to get over myself. This example shows just how important it is for us to be heard, especially concerning those we are close to and whose relationship is important to us.

Old-book knowledge: Know this; my beloved brothers let every person be quick to hear, slow to speak, slow to anger. (Jas 1:19, ESV)

Go with a Blueprint

- Calm down before talking and wait for an opportunity to communicate effectively.
- Listen intently to what your spouse says without interruption.
- Speak with the goal of not putting your spouse on the defensive.
- Ask lots of questions and try to understand thoroughly.
- Remember, listening is an act of love all by itself.

Counselor Notes

Doing a better job of listening to each other in marriage can have a profound positive influence, yet active listening has been taught in marital therapy for years with somewhat limited success. I believe one reason is because, while active listening is effective in communication, it does nothing for couples that have lost love, respect, and friendship because they have lost all motivation to listen. It is not the lack of communicative skill that has strangled their marriage, but the resentments and contempt that have built up in the place of friendship and trust that make communication unappealing.

John Gottman calls attention to this issue in his work where he states, "At the heart of my program is the simple truth that happy marriages are based on deep friendship. By this I mean a mutual respect for and enjoyment of each other's company."[21] This may be why the spoon method is much more effective in premarital counseling. Active listening and effective speaking along with conflict resolution skills are very useful in building friendships and may be better suited for prevention, but the spoon method is also a good way to practice the mechanics of deeper, relationship-building conversation as well.

You cannot build love, accessibility, responsiveness, and an engaging attitude without effective listening and speaking. They are the tools that can help couples develop lifelong relational habits that lead to deep friendship, connection, and bonding, which in turn, as pointed out by Gottman, predict success in making marriage work. We will see in the next chapter that our personal motivations to do well in marriage trump any marital tools we have or could be introduced to.

Questions for Group Discussion

- Why is it a challenge to wait and talk with your husband or wife when emotions have calmed?
- How would really listening to each other improve your marriage?
- Is your husband or wife easily offended and put on the defensive? How do you contribute to the problem?
- What situations do you come across where the spoon method would be helpful?
- What challenges will you face implementing the spoon method in your relationship?
- What are some ways you can use the spoon method to develop friendship in your marriage?

10

Parameters: Motivation

A good blueprint sets the scope or parameters of a project. Understanding the parameters should give sufficient motivation to complete the necessary steps in order to have a completed product as revealed by the blueprint. Of course, if we are not motivated to build a project according to someone else's blueprint, then skipping steps and leaving things undone may be a natural result. If the architect envisions buildings and grounds but we only care about buildings, we may be inclined to not hire a landscaper to finish the project, etc. In the construction world, inspectors generally provide the necessary motivation to follow the approved blueprints, but the best contractors build responsibly for other reasons.

I have learned through the process of counseling hundreds of couples that success or failure in resolving marital conflict and satisfaction or dissatisfaction is determined mainly by the motivation of the individuals involved in the endeavor; their ideas of the finished product apart from the architect's blueprint motivates the actions they will take and the steps they will complete. Therefore, the parameters of success in marriage counseling are set by the individual motivations involved. Highly motivated couples tend to do very well in resolving their issues, and less motivated couples who are on the fence and not so sure about the end product they are seeking tend to do poorly in counseling. Couples that have no motivation usually just part ways, divorce, without even a consideration of working out a solution.

Typical sources of human motivation for marriage oftentimes fail when tested with difficult circumstances. They include personal happiness, financial security, familial obligation, self-fulfillment, sexual attraction, and control. You need motivation that comes from a non-typical source to assure success in much the same way alcoholics in a twelve-step program need a higher power to succeed.

Old-book knowledge: Delight yourself in the Lord, and he will give you the desires of your heart. (Ps. 37:4, ESV)

Pathway to a Loving Relationship

Once we find the right motivation for our marriage, we must learn to stay on the pathway to a loving relationship and avoid losing our balance. I find it helpful to use the acronym PATHWAY in teaching some ideas helpful for maintaining a loving relationship, but first, finding the right motivation to stay on the pathway is instrumental to success.

Having non-typical motivation assures success. Having a good set of tools is good, but even if you have the best counselors, mentors, marriage classes, and therapies at your disposal but are not motivated to succeed or follow a blueprint, all tools will be useless. You can have the best diamond-plated, stainless-steel tool box in your garage with brand-new sets of every kind of tool you can think of inside your box, and it won't help you one bit to complete that household project you never seem to get done, due to lack of motivation. That is why so many contractors have half-finished projects in their own homes; they're not as motivated for the payoff in the end. If you're like me, on the other hand, you can have the crappiest old tool box in the world in your garage and never the right tools, but you somehow manage to get the job done. You're motivated to do the project, so you figure out a way to make it work. It might take you twice as long as an experienced contractor with all the right tools, but you get it done. It's the same way in marriage. If your motivation comes from a powerful source in your life, you will find a way to make it work. If your motivation comes from a weak source, like many of the typical marriage motivations, you will run out of gas and not be able to get the job done, but once you understand the parameters and have sufficient motivation for finding the path to a loving relationship, staying on it will be possible.

Pathway:

P

P is for *protection*. Meeting each other's emotional needs and avoiding the love inhibitors is protection on a loving relationship.

A

A is for *analyze*. You have a marvelous brain capable of looking at things from many different perspectives. You can actually imagine yourself in the place of your husband or wife and see things as they might see things. This goes a long way in shaping our behavior and responses to one another. I try to put myself in other people's shoes in all areas of my life and it tempers my responses. Seeing the world through other people's eyes requires thoughtful consideration, and it is a technique we can and should apply to marriage.

T

T is for time. There is a myth about time that indicates you can plan and spend quality time with someone. I say that there is no such thing as quality time, only time. You can't really plan quality time, it just happens. Have you ever noticed that when you plan a quality activity with someone that it often will not work out as intended, but when you are just hanging out, spending time with someone, all of a sudden, quality moments seem to happen. And as a result, memorable moments are born? These are the moments that we all would like to re-create but seldom can. Have you ever tried to re-create a special moment? Have you been successful? There is no substitute for just spending time with the ones you love, through the good and the bad, quality moments are born, and these moments are never preplanned; although it is necessary to plan time together in specific ways on many occasions. You can't create a marvelous vacation with opportunity for quality moments to happen without some planning.

H

H is for *homeostasis*. Biologically speaking, it is important for living things to be provided environments that are stable. Stable environments are the norm for surviving and flourishing. If your heart begins beating rapidly for any length of time, your body wants it to return to normal and stable as soon as possible. It is a given that you are going to leave the norm or homeostasis from time to time, but like your heart, if you get back to normal in a reasonable amount of time, there is no problem. But if balance is lost and not restored and it beats too fast for too long, you could be in serious trouble. Think of homeostasis in your marriage as a line. Your normal way of being together in relationship is following that line but like a heartbeat you rise above and fall below from time to time. Finding homeostasis in marriage is staying on that pathway of a loving relationship and returning to it quickly when you are diverted. We can all have trials and difficulties that pull us out of that sweet spot, but it isn't the fact that we get pulled out, but how fast we find our way back that determines our long-term viability.

Homeostasis also has a negative aspect. What if our normal flow and routine is not a sweet spot but sour? This is where marriage counseling can help. Routines both good and bad are hard to break, and the way we routinely live and treat each other in marriage is just as difficult. The problem with having a bad routine as your homeostasis is rising above the normal line into a better place, only to succumb to the laws of homeostasis and fall back into your normal unhealthy routines. Marriage counseling should help if you take it as an opportunity to change your normal behaviors and produce a new normal line of homeostasis, but changing normal routines and behaviors takes deliberate action. One couple I previously counseled, Walt and Helena, has had a line of homeostasis in their marriage that over the course of seven years has lead them to the brink of giving up. Walt comes by his overly routine, critical, and unaffectionate ways quite honestly, by virtue of his natural temperament and family upbringing. Helena, on the other hand, has quietly played the martyr and lost her will to continue. They have had their good times in the past, but overall, their normal marriage mode is an unhealthy routine, and this unhealthy routine has left a negative impact, and this negative homeostasis in their marriage can no longer be sustained.

However, marriages with a negative line of homeostasis can be reversed, once Walt and Helena grasped the idea of a routine line with highs and lows, they were able to begin making adjustments that would put their marriage on a sustainable path. Walt began changing his critical responses and deliberately speaking with Helena in caring and affectionate ways. Helena began to appreciate Walt for all of the skill and discipline he did bring into the marriage. They didn't have to shoot for a perpetual honeymoon state, but they did have to maintain a routine in their relationship that would give them both satisfaction and security. This line of homeostasis is a great place for your marriage to be. You can have bad days, falling below the line, and be confident that you'll bounce back up, and you can have great days, soaring above the line and be able to relish them as special moments in your relationship. The goal is to bump up your line. If you don't make changes long enough for them to become permanent, then you are merely visiting a spot above your normal homeostasis line and this line is where you live, so you will eventually end up back there. Make some permanent changes to your relationship that will bump up your line. Now your highs will be higher and your lows will be your old normal. Think about that for a minute.

W

W is for *willingness*. Since we need homeostasis in our marriage, we can't have a marriage without forgiveness. You must be willing to seek forgiveness when necessary and extend forgiveness when asked. Forgiveness puts us back on our normal line when we have fallen below. Going distances without forgiveness will make a permanent change in your marriage that will bump your line downward. A new normal that is lower than before with new highs that are only your old normal. Think about that!

Once again, I look to Walt and Helena for an example. Walt has had his problems keeping a job, and Helena has never been much help with monitoring expenses, but overall, they had a pretty good marriage, except for when the financial strains led them down a path of arguing and complaining. They literally would spend hours explaining arguments they have had trying to win my support for their viewpoint. The problem was that during these arguments, many hurtful things would be said and neither one was willing to forgive and forget or ask for forgiveness. Walt and Helena are now divorced and guess what? They are still arguing and fighting and trying to win support for their side as they deal with the kids and other issues, usually revolving around finances. There is no solution for an unrepentant heart. We must truly be sorry when we wrong others, and we must truly forgive when we have been wronged. Dealing with people with unrepentant hearts on a weekly basis has caused me to really appreciate the necessity for forgiveness in marriage. So much so that I have written the following vows and added them to the traditional wedding vows when performing a wedding ceremony: Walt, do you promise to seek forgiveness and extend forgiveness to Helena when needed throughout your entire life together?

Helena, do you promise to seek forgiveness and extend forgiveness to Walt when needed throughout your entire life together? Without forgiveness, it is impossible to keep your marriage on the pathway to a loving relationship.

A

A is for *addictions*. Eliminate addictions from your life. You cannot maintain a loving relationship when addictions are present. Usually, when we hear the word *addiction*, we automatically think of drugs and alcohol and occasionally sex, but anything that has overtaken you and gets in the way of your interactions with others is an addiction. One of the growing addictions that I have personally experienced while counseling couples today is technology. By technology, I mean cell phones, tablets, Internet, video games, etc. It is becoming more and more common for a husband to spend hours playing video games at the neglect of their wife and kids. Even texting has become so inappropriate between the sexes that relationships are severely threatened at an epidemic level. I once talked with a husband who was emotionally incapable of being intimate with his wife, but was more than content to shut himself in a room and masturbate to video games. Yes, that is what I said, it's not a typo. Addictions and loving relationships don't mix. If you're wondering if something you do is an addiction, just ask yourself if you could give it up if it meant keeping your marriage. If you struggle with that idea, then you are probably addicted. Sometimes affairs are nothing more than an acquired addiction.

Y

Y is for *yes* or *yield*. Just say yes to something. Say yes to positive action. Invest in your marriage with actions that yield a return. Reap what you sow; it is a disaster for a farmer to prepare the ground, plant the seeds, water the field, and care for the crops, and then not have a yield. It is expected if he fails to do those things in preparation, he will have no yield. Diligently approach your marriage with the attitude that you must prepare for a yield. Say yes to action, don't settle for mediocrity, and don't settle for failure, say yes to staying on the pathway.

> *Old-book knowledge*: But if you bite and devour one another, watch out that you are not consumed by one another. (Gal. 5:15, ESV)

Get with a Blueprint:

- Find some untypical motivation
- Protect your marriage
- Use analysis to understand each other's viewpoint
- Plan time for each other
- Bump up your homeostasis line with permanent change
- Be willing to forgive and to ask for forgiveness
- Eliminate addictions
- Invest in your marriage by saying yes to actions that yield returns.

Counselor Notes

Today our culture puts a high value on personal happiness and satisfaction in marriage, but happiness and satisfaction in marriage are an up-and-down rollercoaster ride, unstable at best. When your marriage hits a dip, your motivation is depleted, and the tool box sits idle or gets sold for scrap. My wife and I have been married for almost forty years, and there are days that I just fold my arms and shake my head sideways saying, "No! No! I've had enough, thirty-nine years is enough for anybody." But I have this relationship with God in my life where He begins speaking to me in various ways and he says, "Gary, you know what I want you to do." Then I come to my senses and say, "Okay, Lord, I know what I should be doing." That is powerful, untypical motivation in my life toward my marriage that will never run dry. Serving each other in love is a biblical value and should be strong enough to fuel our motivation.

Time is Not on Our Side

There is no substitute for spending time with our spouse when it comes to improving our marriage, except for spending time with God. Time spent with God is not only time well spent, but time that will directly motivate us to do better in our marriage at every level. Quit waiting for the perfect moment when the sun, moon, and stars are all lined up, and you're feeling extra spiritual. Just stop and spend some time with your Lord, the one who loves you like no other and is always there wanting you to acknowledge Him. So if your marriage is slipping, make more time for each other. If your relationship with God is slipping, spend more time with Him. There is no other way, time must be invested or there will be no return. The moments of your life are fleeting, so don't waste them in being obstinate with God or your spouse. "What is your life? For you are a mist that appears for a little time and then vanishes" (Jas 4:14, ESV).

Homeostasis: Get in the Zone

In our relationship with God, we find homeostasis in allowing the Spirit full access and control of our life. This should be the normal operating zone for those who love God and are called according to His purpose. When we get out of the zone, we must quickly make a correction to avoid long-term damage and ungodly influence.

What about your homeostasis with God? If your relationship with God is bad, and your normal routine is not inviting you into a lasting relationship, maybe you should change the line you are following. Try going to church every Sunday instead of once a month. Try reading your Bible for a few minutes every day instead of once in a while. Begin praying for others instead of yourself. Maybe you don't even have God in your life. Begin by inviting him to be part of what you are doing. Once you create this new line of homeostasis with God, you will continue with highs and lows, but you'll be in a good spot to sustain a close relationship with Him throughout your life.

Willingness

God has forgiven you of an offense that leads to the worst fate a human being can suffer, eternal separation from him. The book of Romans tells us that the penalty of sin is death, not only physical death, but spiritual death as well. Now my mind cannot fully comprehend spiritual death, but if it is the absence of God, and God is light and in Him is no darkness at all, then spiritual death must involve the absence of light. I don't know about you, but that's all I need to know. I don't need to know any more gruesome details to know that it is an unwanted fate. If God has saved you from this kind of fate, why on earth is it not possible for you to forgive one another? Considering the debt that we owe that we can never repay, how could we refuse authentic forgiveness to those that ask for it, especially our spouse? Consider the light in your life and be willing to maintain homeostasis with God, your spouse, and others through forgiveness.

Analyze & Yield

"And let us not grow weary of doing good, for in due season we will reap, if we do not give up." (Gal. 6:9, ESV). Protect your marriage as a farmer protects his crops, analyze each other's viewpoint, and have more understanding, spend time together, as much as you possibly can, build a new and better line of homeostasis to follow, willingly forgive one another as Christ forgave you, eliminate those addictions that are destroying your relationship, and yield a godly blueprint for your marriage. What is the alternative? "Do not be deceived: God is not mocked, for whatever one sows, that will he also reap." (Gal. 6:7, ESV).

Questions for Group Discussion

- What are some underlying motivations that have been driving your attitude in marriage?
- How have you been protecting your marriage?
- How much time do you spend trying to understand your partner's viewpoint? How could doing this improve your marriage right now?
- How much time do you actually spend together with your spouse in meaningful ways? What are some things you could do right now to increase that time? In the future?
- What are some permanent changes you would consider making to bump up your homeostasis line? What are some changes you hope your spouse makes?
- What difference would a willing and forgiving spirit make in your home?
- How are addictions of any kind hindering your marriage?
- In what areas are you willing to say yes and invest in your marriage?

11

Compass: Win the Relationship, Not the Argument

In a blueprint, compasses are used to measure distances, adjoin objects, and draw true circles. A compass has limited margins with a scope and a focal point. On a set of blueprints, we need to judge things relative to each other in revealing ways. Sometimes in marriage, we lose our direction and sense of importance relative to the scope of our overall marriage. Our scope and focal point should always be on winning the relationship, but many times, we make it about not losing an argument or getting our own way. Keeping our compass on winning the relationship as opposed to winning an argument will be useful in creating a marriage true to the blueprint design.

See-Saw Effect

My wife, Fran and I have dubbed the process that couples employ in marriage to focus solely on winning arguments the see-saw effect. In this effect, one person is up and the other person is down. This will ring true at any given time for any given set of circumstances. Some counselors refer to this as the give-and-take process. In this approach, you have to give a little so you can take a little. Compromise can be a good thing, but ultimately, it means giving up something not initially intended to be given up.

Maintaining balance in your marriage is much preferable to taking and giving. You could call this the win-win approach. The husband and the wife must both feel good about the outcome of any disagreement or conflict that arises. When we teeter-totter someone is up and someone is down and based on how we relate together through our personalities, one might find oneself down more often

126

than not. A high phlegmatic married to a high choleric might be in a situation where they are always stuffing down their feelings as they continually acquiesce to their partner's wishes. I don't know about you, but when I was a kid playing with the other boys on the playground at school, my goal on the see-saw was to get the other guy up and then figure out a way to jump off before he could prepare for it. If you're going to be down eventually, you want the other person to pay for being up.

A few years ago, I was working with a couple, Danny and Susan. Danny and Susan were considered one of the more stable Christian couples in our church. Danny was a hard worker, and he kept his family involved in church activities as time allowed, but he ran his home with a somewhat heavy hand. He was a choleric businessman with strong opinions on how to do things, and his wife Susan was a happy-go-lucky, sanguine-phlegmatic; she tried to avoid conflict and be accepted by all. After almost fifteen years of marriage, Susan walked out and left Danny high and dry without warning. When we sat down to talk, Danny conveyed to me how happy they had been and how totally confused he was with the situation. "Susan," he judged. "Must be going off of the deep end. She's gotten spiritually misguided through some evil plot to destroy the family." Eventually, when I talked with Susan, she had a completely different take on the situation, "Our marriage has never been happy. I can't remember the last time Danny considered my feelings when making a decision. I don't want to live like this anymore." You see, Danny didn't have a compass and a blueprint for putting his relationship ahead of his practical, business way of doing things. Susan decided she had been down on the see-saw long enough, and she was getting off only to let Danny come crashing down. Danny had always been up in the relationship, so he was confused to find out that Susan wasn't satisfied with always being on the losing end of their disagreements. She never threw a fit or fussed or demanded her own way, so he figured she was good.

Susan eventually moved back home as they learned how to go about maintaining balance in their relationship.

Maintaining balance is preventing one from getting too high at the other's expense. It's more of a gentle up and down where both keep a positive outlook toward the relationship. There is a so-called give-and-take, but it is more about being happy to give because you've worked out a mutually satisfying solution as opposed to, "I'll give in this time, but I better get my way next time."

My wife, Fran and I, mastered this a few years ago when we couldn't see eye to eye on a family vacation we were planning. I wanted to plan a blowout Alaskan cruise with everyone invited, mostly family and friends; this would be the ultimate large group party ship. As I began to plan and invite, Fran become generally more depressed and non-responsive. In one of my practice-what-you-preach moments, I cracked out the spoon method and began to investigate what was going on. We each listed some of the achievable goals and desires that could be expected from this family vacation. I saw it as a once-in-a-lifetime opportunity to gather many family and friends together. Fran, on the other hand, saw it as an opportunity to spend some quality time with just our boys and their families. She saw my plans as being incompatible with hers, and since I was taking the lead, she was becoming depressed and unhappy. We looked for a win-win solution, so that we could both still be excited about taking this vacation. Together, we decided to stay with the blowout party ship format, but I agreed that the large group party stuff would stay on the ship, and that our quality time with the boys and their families would be achieved by exclusive, on-shore excursions without inviting the others. In the end, we both became excited about the trip, and we both accomplished our goals. We maintained balance, and we didn't destroy the emotional health in our relationship.

Not every situation will have such an easy fix, but if your compass is set for winning the relationship, not arguments, your outcomes and solutions will become more relationship-oriented. You'll be surprised how creatively you can please each other if you set a value and accomplish it together. This actually begins breeding seeds of sacrificial love in the marriage, where both partners look forward to giving up something they want for something their partner wants because they know the mutual goal is balance and they know that their partner would never ask them to give up their needs, wants, and desires selfishly. It's easier to give up something for someone that's not asking than it is to give up something from someone that's scheming for or demanding it.

Scheming and demanding are more about winning the argument, not the relationship, and usually the tactics employed are abusive in nature. We force our selfish will onto our partner. We fail to honor and respect our partner's viewpoint and thus, our partner and we become self indignant, even claiming our behavior is for the good of our partner. Dr. Willard Harley points out, "But disrespectful judgments are not compassionate at all—they're abusive."[22] We convince ourselves that we are helping our partners, not abusing them. Conversely, we should not allow our partner to abuse us in this way. Generally, we do not allow others to treat us in this manner and we should not accept it as normal for our marriage. Allowing your husband or wife to push their point of view on you with these methods is not helping your relationship in the long run.

When I was younger, I spent a good deal of time looking at cars and buying cars with my dad who was a car lover, born in Motown, Detroit, Michigan. Over the years, I learned quite a bit about negotiating car deals while perusing the various car lots with my dad. Most of the time, we were just window shopping, but every now and then, we would actually buy a car, truck, or SUV. We all can learn a little something about negotiating through conflicts in marriage by using the example of the used-car salesman.

When I walk onto a car lot and the salesman sees me approaching, he might have a hidden agenda, he might be interested in selling me the red car on his lot because he makes a good bit more commission on the red car as opposed to the other cars on the lot. But let's say I'm only interested in looking at the blue car. He may be motivated to sell me the red car because he will make more money, but my motivation is not the same as his. Often, car lot owners will motivate their salesmen to move certain cars off of their lot quicker for various reasons. So, as I walk toward the blue car and the salesman approaches, if he yells out, "Hey, come over here, I need you to look at this red car!" And as he gets closer, I say, "No, I'm interested in the blue car." He continues on, "You really need to come over here and look at this red car." Now I will kind of scratch my head and begin to think, *what is this guy's problem? Maybe I should think about leaving this lot and going somewhere else.* He just made a demand of me without any consideration of my wants, needs, desires, or viewpoint. This is mildly abusive and automatically makes me antagonistic to whatever the salesman has to say. In my mind, I am thinking about taking an adverse action by leaving or talking with someone else. Making demands in our relationship without considering your partner's wants, needs, desires, or viewpoints inhibits love, escalates defenses, and opens the door to possible adverse reactions.

Now, assuming that I stay on the car lot and continue to converse with this salesman, trying to communicate my interest in the blue car once again, I could be frustrated further if he continues to push his agenda on me without my input. He might interrupt and say, "You obviously don't know what you're doing if you're interested in the blue car. I am the expert on cars here, and the red car is clearly superior." Now he has just gone from demanding his own way to putting me and my ideas down. Now, it is on! I'm not only going to leave the lot, I may have to have a talk with his manager before I leave. If I'm offended enough, I may never buy a car from that dealership again. In the real world, most of us have figured out that it's not okay to disrespect somebody in this manner. We understand that putting somebody down will not lead to a good negotiation or solution, but for some reason, in marriage, we lose sight of this fact, and we often demand and put down in order to get our own way.

Finally, as I am leaving the car lot without purchasing a vehicle, the disappointed salesperson may lose control and become abusive yelling out, "Thanks for coming by and wasting my time, idiot!" or "Come back and see me again, jerk!" Now, for sure, I will never be doing a car deal with this salesman. We understand this dynamic in the world outside of our marriage, and very seldom does it happen to this degree, but in marriage, it is more common place for such escalations of abuse to occur. Usually, most salesmen will not get upset but want to leave the door open for future negotiations, and they will give you their card and ask you to call again if you change your mind. If they were exhibiting bad behavior during your visit, you would penalize them by not negotiating with them, and they would pay the penalty in the form of lost sales and a sullied reputation.

This is the scenario that you can avoid in your marriage if you decide to focus on winning the relationship and not the argument. The door remains open for future negotiations, no unwarranted demands are made, nobody has been put down and treated as though their viewpoint isn't valid, and hostility is avoided in the relationship. When a call is made, you won't hang up. You may not always get your way, but you will always feel good about your partner. A balance is maintained and the see-saw effect is avoided. Remember, you should never demand your own way with your spouse.

> *Old-book knowledge*: A fool gives full vent to his spirit, but a wise man quietly holds it back. (Prov. 29:11, ESV)

Go with a Blueprint

- Never win an argument at the expense of your marriage.
- Never put getting your own way above the feelings of your spouse.
- Never treat your spouse like they are beneath you.
- Never vent your anger at your spouse.
- Work on a win-win solution to your disagreements.
- Try to keep the see-saw in balance at all times if possible.
- Penalize bad behavior.

Counselor Notes

You should never demean your spouse or their point of view, but you should seek to thoroughly understand them and their viewpoints. "Talk no more so very proudly let not arrogance come from your mouth for the Lord is a God of knowledge, and by him actions are weighed." (1 Sam. 2:3, ESV). Finally, do not allow hostility and indignant behavior into your relationship. There must always be a price to be paid for abusive behavior. For the salesman, the price is a lost sale. If he continued to make sales while being abusive, what incentive would he have to change? And he said to all, "If anyone would come after me, let him deny himself and take up his cross daily and follow me." (Lk 9:23, ESV).

Questions for Group Discussion

- Share a time when you won an argument with your spouse and regretted it later.
- How will your conflicts change if you put the relationship ahead of the outcome?
- Does not winning the argument mean that you lose? Why or why not?
- How do you feel when your spouse puts you down or fails to consider your side of the argument?
- Do you ever have a good outcome when tempers flare? Can you think of some examples?
- What does the see-saw look like in your relationship?
- What would penalizing bad behavior look like? What should the goal be?

12

Basic Specs: Expectations

For builders, the basic specs include all the necessary information to build a building to code. Some codes are standard, like wall studs, sixteen inches on center, and some codes are area specific, based on where you live according to county codes, etc. The basic specs in God's blueprint for marriage include managing our expectations to fit God's purposes. When marriage follows a code different from God's the basic specs, change and the building will not be suitable for his purposes. Our expectations in marriage are greatly influenced by our understanding of the purpose of marriage itself.

Our modern culture tends to put personal happiness at the top of our expectation list. In fact, most of us go into marriage with the false assumption that our personal happiness is the ultimate goal and that nothing else matters. This attitude is the surest way to be unhappy in your marriage. Wrong expectations will bring the potential for failure. A blueprint for marriage that is drawn up, exclusively, to meet the happiness needs of any one particular individual is doomed for failure. It's like building a single family home with the expectation that dozens of families will live in it. It may indeed be able to physically house dozens of families for a while, but ultimately, it will likely break down and be woefully inadequate. If happiness and contentment in marriage are tied to a particular set of circumstances and expected outcomes, the end result is likely to be the onset of resentment and disappointment.

A few years ago, I worked with a couple, Tony and Julie. Tony and Julie were in their thirties, both had been previously divorced, suffering through some significant relationship issues. They dutifully went through premarital counseling with another pastor, doing and saying all the right things, but avoiding the marriage preparation classes offered at our church. Within two months of being married, they ended up in my office with some very tough attitudes toward each other. I explained to them that they must have some unmet expectations of each other because normally, the newness of the relationship alone will carry a newlywed couple for at least a year or so before developing the kind of attitudes that they were already displaying toward each other. After some questioning, they both nodded and admitted to having some unmet expectations of each other.

Julie had been overly stressed, taking care of herself after her previous divorce, and she had hoped that having a partner would reduce her financial stress. Tony, on the other hand, was a full-time student and a part-time worker. Julie had expected that he would begin looking for a better job the moment they got married, and she was unhappy with his feeble attempts to improve his financial outlook. Tony was very angry at Julie's judgment toward him and became even less motivated to contribute more to the family finances. After all, he was already exhausting himself with school and taking care of his eight-year-old son. According to Tony, Julie was not helpful at all and only resented the time he spent with his son. Needless to say, Julie's relationship with his son was strained, and not having children of her own, she was unable to understand why Tony seemed to misplace his priorities, putting his son's needs before hers. She felt devalued and he felt abandoned.

The truth of the matter is whatever concerns you have about your spouse prior to getting married, count on them being magnified times ten the day you say, "I do." This is true because of the increased expectations most of us have about how our spouse should treat us and feel about us. Our expectations of our spouse become obligations they must meet. Tony expected Julie to be a good parent for his son, and she is obliged to do so or risk his disappointment, frustration, and reduced feelings of love. Julie expected Tony to be a better provider, and he is obliged to do so or risk her feelings of irritation and alienation toward him.

The Rub

The rub is even when we do meet each other's expectations and happiness ensues, happiness tends to be fleeting, and a whole new set of expectations is created to feed our endless happiness appetite. Under this growing scrutiny, sooner or later, we will fail to meet each other's expectations. This doesn't mean that we should abandon all expectations of each other, but we shouldn't put such a high price on our expectations always being met. When you need another person to complete you, even a loving spouse, you will always be incomplete and disappointed.

If I come to your house for dinner and afterward, we are sitting around, talking in your living room, and you have left the window open. I might get cold and say, "Brrr...it's getting a little chilly in here." Now I have set you up for failure. If you get up and shut the window, you have only done what any good host would be expected to do. But if you say, "No, actually, I'm a little on the warm side myself," and you don't shut the window, now you're just being a jerk. I had the expectation that you would shut the window, and you were obliged to do so if you wanted to stay in my good graces. On the other hand, if I had been willing to make myself vulnerable to you, I might have said, "Would you please shut the window for me, I'm feeling a little chilly?" That is risky because you might reject me, you might tell me no, and if you do and fail to close the window once I have made myself vulnerable to you, it could hurt my feelings and call into question my own self-worth. On the upside, if you get up and close the window, even if you are actually a little warm, you have committed a deliberate act of love, and you get credit for it. We are actually drawn into closer relationship with each other. I feel valued and you feel benevolent.

Tony could have asked Julie for her help in raising his son and tending to his needs, and Julie would have gotten credit for a deliberate and selfless act of love in doing so. Julie, likewise, could have asked Tony to sacrifice his schooling for a while because of her fragile mental state, and Tony would have gotten credit for deliberately sacrificing his own wants and desires for his wife's well-being. Their pride, fear, and lack of willingness to risk vulnerability with each other caused them to set each other up for failure. Julie would think, *If he really loves me he would see that he needs to do this.* Tony would say, "Any caring wife would go out of her way to be a good mother to my son." Because of their unspoken expectations, they were each saddled with obligations that would remain unmet.

> *Old-book knowledge*: Thus says the Lord: "Cursed is the man who trusts in man *(even a husband or wife)* and makes flesh his strength, whose heart turns away from the Lord. He is like a shrub in the desert, and shall not see any good come. He shall dwell in the parched places of the wilderness, in an uninhabited salt land. "Blessed is the man who trusts in the Lord, whose trust is the Lord. He is like a tree planted by water, that sends out its roots by the stream, and does not fear when heat comes, for its leaves remain green, and is not anxious in the year of drought, for it does not cease to bear fruit." (Jer. 17:5–8, ESV)

Go with a Blueprint

- Be vulnerable with your spouse.
- Be loving to your spouse in their vulnerabilities.
- Keep your expectations in check.
- Draw strength from a more reliable source.

Counselor Notes

Our modern culture tends to put personal happiness at the top of our expectation list, but based on God's DNA of marriage, as discussed earlier, our personal happiness takes a back seat to honoring God, raising godly children, and positively influencing our church, community, and culture. How much consideration is given to honoring God in your marriage? What does it mean to honor God in your marriage? Hopefully, I have given you many things to consider. Have you made your children and family a priority? Are they part of your life's mission? A strong marriage gives you ample resources for a productive life. A troubled marriage will drain all of your resources and strength. Usually leaving nothing left to give God. According to A. W. Tozer, "No man should desire to be happy who is not at the same time holy. He should spend his efforts in seeking to know and do the will of God, leaving to Christ the matter of how happy he should be."[23]

Unspoken expectations are obligations we project onto others, especially those we are in relationship with. When left unmet and unattended, expectations can damage your marriage. God openly communicates his expectation of us: "And you shall love the Lord your God with all your heart and with all your soul and with all your mind and with all your strength.' The second is this: 'You shall love your neighbor as yourself.' There is no other commandment greater than these." (Mk 12:30–31, ESV). When we fail to live up to His expectations, he loves us anyway. "But God shows his love for us in that while we were still sinners, Christ died for us." (Rom. 5:8, ESV). When your strength comes from the grace that God has extended to you through Jesus Christ, you are able to love and accept others, even your spouse, when they don't live up to your expectations. Our expectations, unlike God's, may be flawed anyway. When you draw all of your strength, character, and self-worth from Jesus Christ, in your life you can afford to make yourself vulnerable to others. Even if they reject you, you won't fall apart because you are drawing from your relationship with God.

When we focus our attention on living out our lives under God's expectations of us, we have no time to feel sorry for ourselves and create expectations for those around us, even our husbands or wives. Projected expectations give us a sense of entitlement. You must do this because you owe it to me. Godly-centered relationship is gracious. I will do this for you because I choose to. I want to do this for you because I care, and I'd like to do this for you just because. As opposed to, you should do it because it is expected of you, and you ought to because that is what you're supposed to do. Here are some examples of unmet expectations (you fill in the blanks) and the emotional result in the relationship:

Unmet Expectation	Resulting Emotion
You're supposed to help me with ____	Anger/Hurt
You're supposed to care about ____	Sadness/Unloved
You're supposed to be interested in ____	Rejection/Depression
You're supposed to achieve ____	Disappointment
You're supposed to do this ____	Frustration
You're obligated because ____	Unfulfilled/Emptiness

If all of my strength, character and self-worth come from Him, then I can afford to be rejected by others. If you reject me, I'm still okay. I can go on, I can still love you, and attempt a relationship with you. I don't need you to validate me because Jesus Christ has already done that. If I have to be a little cold at your house because you won't shut the window, I can do it, and I can still love you and not be offended, and I will return to your house on another occasion to continue in relationship. "I can do all things through him who strengthens me." (Phil. 4:13, ESV). If, however, I need you to validate me and prop up my self-worth, I cannot continue with you in the event of rejection. I must withdraw to protect myself, and I can never risk further humiliation or improper treatment at your hand. I cannot return to your house on another occasion without a deep and heartfelt apology, and even then, our relationship will be suspect even if it continues.

To be loved and cherished and validated by your husband or wife is a beautiful thing, but it should never be allowed preeminence over God in fulfilling those emotional needs in your life. As a counselor, if I depend on my clients to accept and validate my self-worth, I become overly concerned about appealing to them in everything that I say and do, being careful not to offend, but if I draw my strength and validation from God and His word, I can freely share for their benefit, not risking or worrying about rejection. I don't rely on a positive reaction from them to uphold my self-esteem. I am free to love without fear of unmet expectations. Love fulfills the law of Christ, and duty or obligation does not. Owe no one anything, except to love each other, for the one who loves another has fulfilled the law. For the commandments, "You shall not commit adultery, you shall not murder, you shall not steal, you shall not covet," and any other commandment, are summed up in this word: "You shall love your neighbor as yourself." Love does no wrong to a neighbor; therefore love is the fulfilling of the law. (Romans 13:8–10)

Questions for Group Discussion

- What are some unmet expectations that have plagued your marriage?
- What are some ways you have attempted to approach your expectations from a position of vulnerability? What was the result?
- What are some examples of responding to your spouse's vulnerability with selfishness and unkindness? Did you feel justified because of your own expectations?
- What are some emotions that your unmet expectations have fostered in your life?
- How will putting your expectations in check improve your marriage?
- Why is putting personal happiness and fulfillment solely on our marriage displeasing to God?
- How does God want us to respond to people in their vulnerabilities?

13

The Architect: Knowing God

God designed the blueprint for marriage that I am encouraging you to follow. If you are able to grasp what God's overall purpose and plan for your life is, then you can also grasp what His blueprint for your marriage is all about. The more you know about the architect, the easier it is to make sense of His blueprint. If you don't want to understand the intricacies of the blueprint, then just skip these last two chapters. Like most blueprints, they can help you build something useful, even if you personally fail to fully understand the architect's vision of the final product. You don't have to fully know and understand God to follow his blueprint for your marriage. You will benefit from His design, and the old-book knowledge that supports His design. If, in fact, you want to better understand the design, then take some time to understand the designer and then you will be better equipped to understand why His design works. His blueprint for marriage is just one of many designs he has created for you.

Understanding God's Will

Knowing God's will is important, but it is not always easy to identify. As individuals, it is easier to follow God's blueprint for our marriage than it is to live out his day-to-day plan for our life, but we will learn that these two ideas are not mutually exclusive. As we live out our life as a married couple, we will always have questions that beg to be answered. It begins with: Should we even get married? And continues with: "Where will we live?" "Where will we work?" "Where will we go to school?" "How many kids should we have?" and on and on and on. We will always have a need to negotiate our understanding of what God's will is for our life, that is, if we are genuinely concerned about what God thinks.

Several years ago, I was at a family camp at Hume Lake Christian Campground, near Fresno, California. This has always been a yearly event for our family. We enjoy good family times along with good music, good food, and good Christian speakers. On this particular weekend, our speaker was Lloyd Shadrach from Fellowship Bible Church in Tennessee. He did a series based on the book of Ruth for the weekend. I enjoyed it immensely and took many notes. Over the years, I have adapted some of what I learned into my presentation for the marriage prep class at our church in presenting the topic of knowing God's will. In the book of Ruth, we normally study what some call, "Kinsman Redeemership" or "loyalty" but buried in the abstracts of Ruth was something more. Something we could take with us into our marriage and apply throughout our life.

Life's Circumstances

The biggest challenge we face in understanding God's will for our life is separating out what God is doing in our life from the circumstances that surround us. We cannot judge what God is doing based on our circumstances. Typically, when things are going very well and things are going our way we say things like, "God is with us, God is blessing us, God is smiling on us or God is good." When things seem to be going very bad, we say things like, "Where is God?" "God has left me, God doesn't care, and God is punishing me." But our circumstances do not dictate what God is doing in our life or God's ultimate plan for us.

If circumstances were a good measure of God's presence in our life, we might be compelled to say: many men of God whose stories are recorded in the pages of the Bible did not have God with them. For instance, the prophet Jeremiah was called as a young man to speak for God. God told him to tell the nation of Israel to repent and turn from false gods, or they would fall into captivity in Babylon. Oh, and by the way, Jeremiah, you will be beaten, thrown into a pit, and spend most of your life imprisoned, and ultimately, no one will listen to you, and your people will end up in captivity anyway.

Jeremiah even told God at one point that he felt like he was getting ripped off. When you examine the circumstances of Jeremiah's life, you will be tempted to conclude that God was not with him. Jeremiah had to have doubted at many points in his life, but as we look back and see what God was doing we understand that God was with Jeremiah and did have a plan for his life. Jeremiah didn't understand all of God's purposes in his life circumstances. He couldn't have known that we would still be talking about him and his circumstances thousands of years later. He could only see and experience the circumstances right in front of his eyes and trust that God in His sovereignty was in control. Current circumstances are never a surefire way to judge what God may or may not be doing in your life.

> *Old-book knowledge*: The steadfast love of the Lord never ceases; his mercies never come to an end; they are new every morning; great is your faithfulness. "The Lord is my portion," says my soul, "therefore I will hope in him." (Lam. 3:22–24, ESV)

Three Things That Must Be Understood about God's Will for Your Life

1. Ninety percent of God's blueprint for your life has already been revealed to you in the pages of the Bible.

Our long time family Pastor, Rob Zinn, used to say as he held up the Bible in one hand, "Black ink on white paper!" Let me ask you a question, "If 90 percent of God's plan for your life has already been revealed to you in the pages of the Bible, why should God supernaturally reveal the other 10 percent to you if you're not actively striving to seek out God's truth and live by his word and follow his principles?" We get most of what God wants for our life in His revealed word to us. By seeking out and obeying His principles for living, we open the door to a more supernatural encounter and direction from Him.

The senior pastor at my previous church, Matt Brown, is always saying things like, "God spoke to me, I heard God, God told me."

142

Back then, as a fellow staff member, occasionally people would come to me and ask, "What does pastor Matt mean when he says that God spoke to him? God has never spoken to me, so I don't understand what he's talking about." I would usually respond with, "When someone says that God spoke to them, it can mean one of two things. One, they are trying to set themselves up as an authority to get you to follow them in some way, and if what God is telling them goes against the written word of God, I am not only skeptical, but prefer to run as far from that person as possible and never drink the Kool Aid. The voice speaking to them is not from God and is most likely demonic, or the person is an outright deceiver or, at the very least, disingenuous.

Two, they are actively seeking out God's principles for their life in His Word, and because they are striving to seek out God's truth and live by His Word, God is revealing new things to them in supernatural and Spirit-influenced ways. I believe the latter is the case with Pastor Brown. He is striving to live a life obedient to God's word, and as God's chosen leader of his church, God continues to reveal things to him in supernatural ways. I'm not sure I would want to follow a pastor that was not hearing from God on a regular basis.

So, why should God reveal to you supernaturally what has not already been revealed if you are not striving to know and obey those things that have already been revealed for your life? Why should he reveal answers to your questions: Is this the person I should marry? Is this the job I should take? Is this the house we should live in? Is now a good time to start a family? What church should we attend? There are many questions in our life that we need God to speak in to. Get into God's word, discover those things He has already revealed, His principles and precepts, and begin living out those principles in authentic ways and see how God will speak to you in other significant, spiritual and supernatural ways.

2. Most of God's blueprint for your life is not visible in the present.

God's provision for your life is something that can only be fully seen when looking back. Usually, as we navigate through life circumstances we find ourselves unaware and not understanding exactly what God is doing in our life. Often, though, with the passage of time, we are able to look back and see God's hand on the situation and begin to fully understand how God provided and used those circumstances as part of his providential will for our life. When my wife, Fran, and I were married almost forty years ago, both of us at eighteen years of age, we had no idea or even the ability to understand how God would one day use us as marriage mentors, teachers, and spiritual leaders. We can look back, however, and see the various circumstances and challenges, difficulties, and highlights we faced as a couple and with our family and say to ourselves, "Look what God did! Look how God used everything in our life to bring us to this point. He knew where we were going even when we didn't." Yes, we can clearly see God's hand by looking back. Our challenge and our faith is a mandate to trust in God and have faith that he is working in our life. We must always be looking forward to God's provision in God's time and in God's way. God's past provision can be a great source of comfort for difficult circumstances occurring in the present.

3. Sometimes God's plan is none of our business

Sometimes, we just need to let God be God. God is in control, and he will accomplish his purposes. He has a plan for your life and a plan for my life, and who are we to question that plan? The prophet Jeremiah thought that he was getting ripped off by God when he found out that he was investing his life in proclaiming God's word to a people that were never going to listen. He would've never signed up for such a task. That would kind of be like God telling Fran and I, "I want you to do premarital counseling with hundreds of couples over many years of your life. Oh, and by the way every single one of those couples will have a marriage that ends in divorce." "Sign me up God. That's what I'd like to do with my life. Waste it on undeserving people that will not listen to what I have to say or learn anything of lasting value. Yes, that's it sign me up!" We lack the information, foresight, understanding, and ability to do God's planning for him. So let's let God be God and not try to stand in the way of His plan.

The Story in the Book of Ruth

In the book of Ruth, Elimelech, Naomi, and the boys, Mahlon and Chilion, left God's revealed will in a search for better circumstances. There was a famine in Israel, a bad circumstance; they needed to move their family to Moab in order to eat. Right? It must have been God's will because in Moab, the circumstances were better and they continued there. Elimelech eventually died, but the boys found wives, Orpah and Ruth, so the family continued on in Moab for ten years. They were not in God's will or following His blueprint. They had the books of Moses, they had God's word, they knew the traditions of Israel, and they knew that they had left the promised land. They weren't living out God's principles and revealed plan for their life. They didn't wait for God's provision, and they didn't accept God's blueprint and purpose for their life. Moab was a country whose people were descendants of Lot. They were considered enemies of Israel and banned from the congregation of the Lord. They worshiped pagan gods and even sacrificed their children to their gods, making them detestable, as a nation, in the sight of God.

Subsequently, when the boys died, another bad circumstance, Naomi judged that God was not with her anymore and, in fact, was against her. She judged what God was doing in her life based on circumstances. In this case, however, the facts show that God didn't even show up until the circumstances went bad. Naomi surmised that God was with her in Moab when the circumstances were good, but when the circumstances went bad, God was against her. So she said to them, "Do not call me Naomi; call me Mara, for the Almighty has dealt very bitterly with me. I went away full, and the Lord has brought me back empty. Why call me Naomi, when the Lord has testified against me and the Almighty has brought calamity upon me?" (Ru 1:20–21, ESV).

This story of Ruth is perfect for helping us understand the truth: we cannot judge what God is doing based on circumstances. Ironically, a man by the name of Elimelech, whose name means "God is my king," moved his family from Bethlehem, meaning "house of bread," to feed them. The story ends up back in Israel, where, guess what? They have food and people are eating. Didn't Israel just dry up and blow away in the famine? Didn't Elimelech and Naomi and the boys have to leave the promise land in order to survive? It seems not. From this, we should learn that the best we can do through bad circumstances is continue in God's revealed will, following his principles, and wait for his provision, accepting His plan for our life.

It turns out in this story that Ruth is a big part of God's plan, and we can learn much about negotiating circumstances, and God's plan in our life by looking at her life. Before we continued to be too hard on Elimelech, Naomi, and the boys, we can see that they must have told Ruth and Orpah about the one true and living God of Israel based on Ruth's testimony to Naomi. But Ruth said, "Do not urge me to leave you or to return from following you. For where you go I will go and where you lodge I will lodge. Your people shall be my people and your God my God. Where you die I will die, and there will I be buried. May the Lord do so to me and more also if anything but death parts me from you." (Ru 1:16–17, ESV). Ruth made a decision to make God the Lord of her life and to follow His principles, wait for His provision, and accept his purpose for her life regardless of the circumstances. Orpah, on the other hand, did what most of us would've done given the same set of circumstances. She did what was expedient for her in the moment. Her decision was much like Elimelech's in moving the family to Moab. The prospects for a single woman traveling to a foreign country without a husband were not ideal. It made logical sense to stay in the pagan country and marry a pagan husband that would guarantee your future and safety, at least from a temporal physical standpoint.

Who's the Boss of You?

Making Christ the Lord of your life requires you to give up the endless chase for good circumstances and to trust and believe in a God who is in control and will accomplish his plan and purpose for life as you live by his Word. Ruth had settled the issue of Lordship in her life. Ask yourself the question, "Who is the boss of you?" Is the Lordship of your life personally settled? When the Lordship of your life is settled, when God is the boss of you, certain decisions in life are already made for you. I will not deliberately cause a divorce or be unfaithful to my wife because God has already determined that this is not His plan for my life. I will worship the Lord on Sundays or Saturdays because God has already determined that this is His will for my life. However, if I am the boss of me, I am likely to do whatever seems best for me in the moment, like Orpah leaving God's will and returning to a pagan life in Moab.

Fran and I once counseled a young couple, Brian and Cheryl. Brian was a junior lawyer with a local law firm, and Cheryl was a physician's assistant. They were living together before marriage and felt that they were in God's will and that God approved of their situation. They reasoned that they had already made a commitment toward marriage because of their engagement, and the only reason they were living together was because they wanted to take advantage of a great deal on a house. They were young professionals and felt the need to be rewarded for their hard work and schooling. This particular house they would not have been able to afford if they continued to live separately, paying double rents. They would soon be married and felt somewhat practical in their decision. The fact that they were living together prematurely must be okay with God, they reasoned to themselves, because of how great the circumstances had turned out for them. The house was great and the deal on it was unmatchable in their minds, their jobs were good, and Brian received a promotion, everything was coming up roses, and they had the money and plans for an extraordinarily upscale wedding ceremony on the horizon. God must be looking down and smiling on them. After all, they had made a commitment toward marriage, and so this must all be part of God's grand plan and blueprint for them.

Trust the Designer

The truth is that God prefers obedience to sacrifice and God's provision rests in Israel, not Moab. God wants us to make him the Lord of our life and he wants us to trust in Him. God can provide a house when he is ready for us to have one, just like God provided food for Israel. His provision will never come outside of His principles and purpose. Sometimes, surviving the famine is just letting God be God. He has not hidden His character from us and everything that we do know about God and His purposes, he has revealed to us in the Bible. When Ruth began to glean for food in the field of Boaz, she was following God's Word, and God's established welfare system for the poor. Ruth was blessed for following God's Word in this way, and Boaz was also blessed for following God's Word in this way. There may very well have been other wealthy land owners that didn't leave anything for the poor to glean, but meticulously collected it all for themselves against God's will. They may have missed out on God's provision for their life unlike Boaz in this story.

Ruth's ability to trust and wait on the Lord landed her in God's favor. "The Lord repay you for what you have done, and a full reward be given you by the Lord, the God of Israel, under whose wings you have come to take refuge!" (Ru 2:12, ESV). God's will for your life is moving and dynamic. Are you anticipating God's provision and providence in your life? Ruth's actions were based on trust in the Lord. How are your actions determined? Doing God's will is often just doing what's right in the moment. If you're like me, you spend much time telling yourself of all the great things that you want to accomplish for the Lord tomorrow. But when it comes to doing what's right in front of you in the moment, we fail. Ruth just did what she knew to do and she kept at it until God provided. This helped her to remain faithful over time, but she was also faithful in the present as she went to the fields to glean and went to the threshing floor to seek God's will and provision for her life. And she replied, "All that you say I will do." (Ru 3:5, ESV). Do what is right in front of you for the Lord today. Don't be that great man or woman of God, "Someday!"

Go with a Blueprint

- Seek to know and understand God and His Word.
- Trust the architect by following his design, not your own.
- Remain faithful to the process.
- Act now, not tomorrow.

Counselor Notes

So the question still remains, "How can we know God's unrevealed plan and purpose for our life?" Don't ask if something is God's will, but ask, "How is my relationship with God?" "For it is God who works in you, both to will and to work for his good pleasure." (Phil. 2:13, ESV). If you're walking with God, and you have a good relationship with Him, you can trust your instincts, but if you're not walking with God and your relationship is broken, you cannot trust anything going on in your own mind. Sometimes, even when we feel like we have a good relationship with God, we make decisions that seem to be mistakes. I'm sure that Jeremiah felt that way. But we never know when God is moving us from point A to point B, and he really wants us to go to point C, D, E and F first. That is why we should strive to have a heart that seeks after God and simply trust him, having faith in what he will accomplish.

> Blessed is the man who walks not in the counsel of the wicked, nor stands in the way of sinners, nor sits in the seat of scoffers; but his delight is in the law of the Lord, and on his law he meditates day and night. He is like a tree planted by streams of water that yields its fruit in its season, and its leaf does not wither. In all that he does, he prospers. (Ps. 1:1–3, ESV)

Questions for Group Discussion

- How can knowing the architect help you with following his blueprint?
- In what ways have you judged what God is doing in your life based on your circumstances?
- How have you been able to look back and see God working in your life? In your marriage?
- How will knowing God's will help your marriage?

- What issues are going on in your life right now where you need to let God be God?
- Has the Lordship of your life been settled? If so, what is preventing it? Who is the boss of you?
- Explain your current relationship with God? Can you trust yourself? Why or why not?

14

Engineering: Sexual Intimacy through Spiritual Discipline

Detailed plans must be engineered if they are to be used in a practical way for constructing a building. The engineering specs determine if a plan is feasible and if it will hold up in a safe and useful manner. It would be of little use to attach beams with brackets and bolts of insufficient strength to carry the necessary weight. Marriage requires a sexual connection to properly bear the relational weight of marriage in God's design. In God's blueprint for marriage, physical intimacy is the necessary element to support the kind of oneness relationship that God had in mind. Sex is so important that God did not envision a marriage relationship without it. In marriage, sex and relationship are one and the same. Mankind has ripped sex from its godly created environment and made it all about orgasm and physical pleasure, but God has always intended it to be exclusive to the marriage relationship, a special part of marriage, making it different from any other relationship in your life. Developing sexual intimacy in our marriage can be much the same as developing our spiritual relationship with God. Our marriage is physical and so the disciplines of building marital intimacy are physical. Our relationship with God is spiritual, and so the disciplines for building intimacy with God are spiritual.

> *Old-book knowledge*: There are heavenly bodies and earthly bodies, but the glory of the heavenly is of one kind, and the glory of the earthly is of another. (1 Cor. 15:40, ESV)
>
> God is spirit, and those who worship him must worship in spirit and truth. (John 4:24, ESV)

Spiritual Discipline

Spiritual discipline is the special part of our relationship with God that symbolizes oneness in much the same way sex symbolizes oneness in our marriage. Spiritual disciplines include daily devotions, intentional encounters, and lingering or long-term involvement, producing immediate and long-range benefits for the individual in his or her relationship with God as well as lasting change in godly character and influence. According to Henry Nouwen, a contemplative chaplain and author, required reading for pastoral counselors,

"A Spiritual life without discipline is impossible. Discipline is the other side of discipleship. The practice of spiritual discipline makes us more sensitive to the small, gentle voice of God."[24] It is possible to improve our physical intimacy and sensitivity in marriage by developing it in much the same we develop our intimacy and sensitivity to God.

Daily Devotion

Develop a ten-minute daily devotional. The spiritual discipline of daily devotion is reading God's word, devotionals, study guides, reference notes, journaling, and prayer. For women, this usually has the immediate benefit of developing a responsive relationship with God, and for men, it creates intentionality with God. Long–range, she becomes a devoted follower of Christ, and he becomes a developing spiritual leader. For both, it means lasting godly character.

The spiritual discipline of daily devotion can teach us how to practice daily physical intimacy. Like our daily devotion to God, the amount of time is not the issue, but the daily devotion to the activity. Ten minutes per day is an adequate practice and beginning point for your devotion to God, and spending at least ten minutes per day in physical contact with your spouse is also a necessary practice for building physical intimacy into your relationship with each other. Practice physical touch, being together in close proximity along with simple conversation for at least ten minutes a day.

Old-book knowledge: Therefore, as you received Christ Jesus the Lord, so walk in him, rooted and built up in him and established in the faith, just as you were taught, abounding in thanksgiving. (Col. 2:6–7, ESV)

Daily Devotion in Our Sex Life:

Kindness, tenderheartedness, and a forgiving attitude will thrive in an environment where daily devotion is given to physical contact between husband and wife. Like your daily devotion with God, it does require giving up daily of yourself, time needs to be planned and set aside for this activity every day. Remember, we call this a discipline leading to relationship. Men need to understand that this daily activity is not foreplay, and women need to understand that developing responsiveness and spontaneity is crucial to developing satisfying physical intimacy with their husbands. This daily encounter can become a sexual encounter at the prompting of the wife. This is what spontaneity is all about, a spontaneous response that is not the normal or expected response. It is somewhat impossible for it to be spontaneous at the prompting of the husband because men are almost always spontaneous when it comes to sex. When men become more spontaneous to dishing out affection, without sex, as a daily devotion, they will seem more spontaneous and less brash to their wives. The husband should always approach this time as nonsexual relational affection and be pleased when his wife initiates more. The immediate benefit for her is relational intimacy and for him the receiving of love. Long-range, she becomes more aggressive sexually, and he becomes more aggressive relationally. She feels secure in the connection, and he feels honored. I have worked with several couples who were able to restore their sexual connection after years of sexless marriage by beginning with this simple commitment to daily physical devotion. However, in about 25 percent of marriages, the roles are reversed, and the women are more aggressive sexually and spontaneity must be initiated by the husbands. In either case, the need for physical touch is built into our essence from birth and continues throughout our lives. The need for infants to be touched and held for normal development is widely documented and researchers are beginning to have a deeper understanding of how our emotional health is tied to our physical well-being and how our physical well-being is often influenced by physical touch, proximity and human interaction.[25]

Despite what our experience or lack of experience teaches us and despite what our families, culture, and the media teach us, women need sex for a healthy marriage and men need nonsexual affection. We can see it in God's blueprint: submission, love, and sex are all part of a complete, God-honoring, marriage union, propagating safety, security, honor, and respect. It's no wonder that many couples are discovering that long-term satisfaction in marriage fits this same model. When we begin with God's creative design, we begin with wisdom. When all else fails, we can still follow the directions.

Do not attempt to follow a plan without the engineering of daily devotion.

Weekly Devotion

Set aside a time to worship God weekly. Some churches offer worship on both Saturdays and Sundays. Historically, the church has worshipped on Sundays in honor of the resurrection of our Lord and Savior, Jesus Christ, who rose from death to life on the first day of the week. Only a historic event of this magnitude could cause a change from worshipping on the Sabbath, Saturday, to worshipping on the first day of the week, Sunday. The principle, however, is the same no matter what day of the week you choose to worship. God created the universe and everything in it in six days and rested on the seventh. We honor and worship Him by setting aside one day a week to recognize Him as Creator and Savior.

Today, in most churches, we consider worship to be the music. We talk about the worship bands and songs and we debate worship styles: contemporary, traditional, nontraditional. We choose choirs or worship teams, hymnals, or music slides. We often rate our experience as being worshipful or not based on our emotional response to the music. But true worship is not examining personal emotion or feelings about our church experience, nor is it a good feeling about how well the preacher communicated or entertained us, but it is the discipline of setting aside one day a week to honor God, whether we feel like it or not. God gives us six days to plan and live our lives, and as our Creator, he wants us to set aside one day for Him. True worship is not an option for a godly man or woman. We worship God by showing up weekly, taking time from our own lives and schedules to give it to God. Don't get me wrong, doing a good job at singing and communicating is part of our worship offering as well, but worship is a discipline exercised from us to God, not an emotional high implanted from God to us.

There is no reason to a have a seven-day week, except, like marriage, it is a very symbolic lesson for us in understanding our relationship with God. Most scales established for time measurement, including hours, minutes, seconds, days, months, and years are based on the created universe around us, but the week has no real relationship to the universe around us, like the twenty-four-hour day being based on the rotation of the earth, etc. The week is given to us symbolically to measure God's working with men. The Soviets toyed with the idea of changing the seven-day week in the early twentieth century, but eventually defaulted back to the seven-day week. Clearly, God sees value in the use of a weekly devotion for worship. Jack Hayford, Senior Pastor Emeritus of Church on the Way in Van Nuys, California, points out, "My praise and worship will determine the dimensions of my forward advancement along the pathway of discipleship. I will advance no further than my heart of worship allows me. I may become deep in knowledge and brilliant in spiritual insights, but my worship before God will determine my true stature as a son or daughter and my maturity as a growing servant-disciple."[26]

Him and Her Benefits of Weekly Devotion

An intentional encounter with God in worship on a weekly basis as a spiritual discipline has an immediate benefit for her in her closeness with God, and an immediate benefit for him as he is strengthened by God. The long-range benefit for her is a peace through all of life's circumstances that can only come from her relationship with God and for him as he is challenged into service. This discipline will create a lasting change in him and her and in their overall spiritual health and well-being.

Weekly Devotion in Our Sex Life:

To improve our sexual connection, we also need to practice the discipline of intentional weekly encounters. We should set aside at least one day a week to have an intentional sexual encounter with our spouse.

> How beautiful and pleasant you are, O loved one, with all your delights! Your stature is like a palm tree, and your breasts are like its clusters. I say I will climb the palm tree and lay hold of its fruit. Oh may your breasts be like clusters of the vine, and the scent of your breath like apples, and your mouth like the best wine. It goes down smoothly for my beloved, gliding over lips and teeth. I am my beloveds, and his desire is for me. (Song of Sol. 7:6–10, ESV)

Notice how the exclusivity of sex in the marriage relationship adds to the sexual excitement.

Some might complain that scheduling a day for sex is not very romantic, but for most guys, this will never be a problem. In fact, for most husbands, knowing there is a set time for this encounter that will not be susceptible to his wife's mood or sense of tiredness, etc. will be exhilarating, and the same is true for the 25 percent or so of wives that are more sexually aggressive than their husbands. Remember, spontaneity will be built into your physical relationship as you practice daily devotion, and this will make the weekly encounter pleasant for the wife, or less sexually motivated husband as well, giving both the husband and wife a sense of control and excitement over their own sexuality and the physical relationship with their spouse. The husband doesn't have to deal with rejections, and the wife doesn't feel used or neglected. Men will continue to grow relationally when practicing these disciplines, and women need to remember that this weekly encounter is not a courtesy, but a godly discipline for them as well. If the wife treats this weekly encounter as a courtesy or favor for the husband, it will have the same negative effect as the husband treating the daily intimacy devotion as an opportunity for foreplay leading to sex. It defeats the purpose.

> *Old-book knowledge*: Enjoy life with the wife whom you love, all the days of your vain life that he has given you under the sun, because that is your portion in life and in your toil at which you toil under the sun. Whatever your hand finds to do, do it with your might, for there is no work or thought or knowledge or wisdom in Sheol, to which you are going. (Eccles. 9:9–10, ESV)

Him and Her Benefits of a Weekly Sexual Encounter

The immediate benefit of a weekly encounter for the wife is an opportunity to show a deliberate act of love to her husband, and for the husband, it is a sense of release and deepening affection for his wife. As a long-range benefit, sex becomes more physically stimulating for the wife, and sex becomes more relationally stimulating for the husband. Both will experience a lasting change in the development of a more loving connection, and as Solomon points out in our old-book knowledge, life is too short and hard in many ways to not enjoy each other as husband and wife to the fullest.

Spiritual Discipline: Lingering, Long-Term Involvement

The spiritual devotion of lingering involvement involves activities on a monthly, quarterly, or yearly basis; serving in an area of ministry that you have been called to through the leading of the Holy Spirit, your ministry or involvement with and for the body of Christ. We begin our journey down the road to a vital transforming faith when we use the time, talents, and resources that God has given us for the benefit of others and His kingdom. I have learned that the only way to assure a vital marriage relationship is to follow God's blueprint and allow our marriage to be an ambassadorship representing Christ and His kingdom. I have discovered that couples who come into counseling and improve usually end up back in trouble down the road if they don't practice the discipline of lingering involvement, using their marriage for God's kingdom as help and strength to others. At our church, we put a lot of time and effort into not only helping couples have a better marriage, but also in helping them to become ambassadors. This is why, if we do nothing else that centers on marriage in our churches but to raise up and train, mentor couples to help other couples that are hurting, we are fulfilling our obligation to God.

> *Old-book knowledge*: Bear one another's burdens, and
> so fulfill the law of Christ. (Gal. 6:2, ESV)

Some of the strongest mentor couples that I have personally worked with have been through the fire in their own marriages and emerged out the other side as ambassadors serving Christ. In some cases, there was a time when divorce was imminent, but with help from their church and other godly influences, they were able to overcome some significant issues. Most have never looked back. Why? Because they fixed their marriage so well the first time that they don't have any problems. No, I don't believe that to be the case, but I believe it is because they turned their success into lingering, long-term involvement in helping others. Now, through their leadership, many couples are being helped, and they have greatly influenced others, leaving a lasting legacy as well. Teachers always learn more than their students, and this same concept holds true for marriages. If you want ongoing success in your marriage, become ambassadors for Him, it's the godly model, and it works every time.

Him and Her Benefits of Long-Term or Lingering Involvement

Practicing the discipline of lingering involvement in your spiritual life provides benefits as well. The immediate benefit for her in this spiritual discipline is a greater sense of belonging, and for him, it is much needed accountability. To be a good spiritual leader, the husband must not only be in submission to Christ, but also to the spiritual authority that Christ has placed over him within the context of the church. The long-range benefit for her is an increased attitude of submission, and for him, it is an increased ability to love. The lasting change for both of them will be a transforming faith, transforming themselves and others.

Lingering, Long-Term Involvement in Our Sex Life

The physical intimacy discipline of lingering involvement includes spending time together as a couple in planning, dreaming and problem solving with retreats, escapes, getaways, dates, and vacations. This will vary from couple to couple based on economic ability and time commitments, but to default to zero is not acceptable in any situation. Fran and I would escape on mini weekends and retreats whenever we could swing it financially. Sometimes, that was only once a year, but we made it happen. Other times, it was just a coffee date and an hour alone while the kids were away at school, Grandma's, or a friend's home, etc. Spending a day together monthly would be another approach or a weekend away per quarter. During these times, sex should not be a sidebar but a central focus. Also, include relational affections, friendship and caring gestures if possible. For couples that are financially challenged, a friendly couple to watch the kids for you while you stay home alone for a few hours will do. Be creative; where there is a will, there is a way. But put it on the calendar, because just like your involvement at church, if you don't commit and put it on the calendar, you won't do it. Engineer your plans, or you can't build anything, especially something as detailed and fragile as the sexual connection in your marriage relationship.

His and Her Benefits of Lingering, Long-Term Sexual Devotion

The immediate benefit for her will be relief from life circumstances and security in her marriage, and for him, a hopeful attitude for the future of their relationship. The long-range benefit for her will be contentment with herself and for him, a renewed excitement and energy for life in general. The lasting change for both will be a deepening commitment and lifelong bond to each other.

Go with a Blueprint

- Plan ten minutes a day with God in some kind of Bible reading and payer.
- Plan ten minutes a day in close physical contact with your husband or wife.
- Plan a weekly time to worship the Lord with other believers.
- Plan a weekly time of sexual connection with your husband or wife.
- Plan a special work of service for the Lord on a monthly, quarterly, or yearly basis.
- Plan a special time together as a couple on a monthly, quarterly, or yearly basis.

Counselor Notes

This plan for building sexual connection by comparing it to spiritual discipline is meant to help those that are struggling in the area of sex in their marriage. So, if it isn't broke, don't fix it. However, many couples are having difficulty in this area, nevertheless, are in denial. Couples seldom share their dissatisfaction sexually until it surfaces in other damaging ways; they never fully understand the need for sexual connection as part of a satisfying relationship in marriage. Once you realize the godly and spiritual connection between sex and relationship in marriage, you can practice these disciplines that will enhance your relationship with God and each other. The alternative is no relationship or poor relationship. Sometimes, practicing spiritual discipline with God seems mechanical and unfeeling, but not practicing spiritual discipline guarantees an unnatural and non-charismatic relationship with God. The same is true for your marriage.

If God is working in your life, the call is a call to action. The call to action in your marriage is to investigate, understand, and implement God's design. It is perfect and it never fails. Remember, creation matters. If God has a plan and a purpose, then he must have a design that we can follow, even if God is not part of your life, following His blueprint for marriage will benefit you. This is accomplished in much the same way as following the physical and natural laws around us; it benefits those that order their lives around them. Defying them will only lead to struggle and failure. Imagine building a home with no roof in Seattle, or a home with no ventilation in Arizona. A marriage that ignores God's design will have the same kinds of challenges to face. I hope that these sessions I've laid out will help you in your investigation and understanding of God's design. The implementation is on you!

Questions for Group Discussion

- What are some road blocks you experience in your daily devotion to God? With your spouse?
- Have you ever considered your church attendance in itself as worship? Why or why not? What does it mean to be a consumer Christian?
- How well do you think a weekly planned time for sex will play in your marriage? What are the benefits? Drawbacks?
- What involvement beyond attendance do you have at your church?
- How often do you plan time away together as a couple? What are the benefits? Drawbacks?

Final Thought

There are evil forces at work in the world, dominions and powers. Your marriage is part of God's overall strategy to win the battle that rages on between good and evil. Unfortunately, God's enemy knows His strategy and works hard to thwart it whenever possible.

Old-book knowledge: For we do not wrestle against flesh and blood, but against the rulers, against the authorities, against the cosmic powers over this present darkness, against the spiritual forces of evil in the heavenly places. (Eph. 6:12, ESV)

In some countries, girls are forced into marriage at a very young age. It would be hard to argue that a model of this kind fits God's blueprint design for marriage as a unifying relationship of co-authority. Wife abandonment and murder is also a problem in economically depressed regions. These and other divergent forms of marriage that may create harm to humans can help us understand that God does have a practical purpose for His marriage blueprint. When we don't follow it, we encourage human tragedy at varying levels.

My goal here has not been to provide intellectual or scientific proof that God's design for order and community is a more prosperous and beneficial way to live, though I think a good argument could be made, but I merely want to point out that God has a blueprint design for us to follow. It behooves us to acknowledge the Creator, if he wants something to be a certain way, why should we be so willing to argue with Him, or so careless as to not know? Now, you know!

Where were you when I laid the foundation of the earth? Tell me, if you have understanding. (Job 38:4, ESV)

Notes

1. James Q. Wilson, *The Marriage Problem: How Our Culture Has Weakened Families* (New York: HarperCollins Publishers Inc., 2002), 5.
2. Emerson Eggerich, *Love and Respect: The Love She Desires Most, The Respect He Desperately Needs* (Nashville: Thomas Nelson Publishing, 2004), 113.
3. Wilson, 104–105.
4. Wilson, 220.
5. John M. Gottman, *The Seven Principles For Making Marriage Work* (New York: Three Rivers Press, New York, 1999), 19.
6. Bowling Green State University, National Center for Marriage and Family Research, July 2013.
7. Wilson, p. 53.
8. Wilson, PFD.
9. Tim LaHaye, *Spirit Controlled Temperament* (Wheaton: Tyndale House Publishers, 1966).
10. Marita Littauer, *Wired That Way* (Ventura: Regal Books from Gospel Light Publishers, 2006).
11. Marita Littauer, "Personality Assessment Tool" (Ventura: Regal Books from Gospel Light, 2006).
12. Willard Harley, *His Needs, Her Needs* (Grand Rapids: Revell, 2011).
13. Emerson Eggerich, *Love and Respect: The Love She Most Desires, The Respect He Desperately Needs* (Nashville: Thomas Nelson, 2004).

14. Hart, *Safe Haven Marriage: Building a Relationship You Want to Come Home To* (Nashville: W Publishing Group, 2003).

15. Willard Harley, *Love Busters: Protecting Your Marriage From Habits That Destroy Romantic Love* (Grand Rapids: Revell, 2008).

16. Shaunti Feldhahn, *For Women Only: What You Need to Know About the Inner Lives of Men* (Doubleday Press, 2004).

17. Norman Wright, *Communication the Key to Marriage* (Glendale: G/L Publications, 1974).

18. Tommy Nelson, "Song of Solomon Marriage Conferences."

19. Sue Johnson, *Hold Me Tight: Seven Conversations for a Lifetime of Love* (Boston: Little Brown & Co., 2008).

20. Clarks, *Passion That Lasts a Lifetime.*

21. John Gottmon, *The Seven Principles for Making Marriage Work,* 19.

22. Willard Harley, *Love Busters: Protecting Your Marriage from Habits That Destroy Romantic Love* (Grand Rapids: Revell, 2008), 74.

23. W. Tozer, published by the children of A. W. Tozer, *Of God and Men* (Chicago: Moody Publishers, 2015).

24. Henry J. Nouwen, *The Wounded Healer* (New York: Doubleday, 1972).

25. Tiffany Field, *Touch* (MIT Press, 2003).

26. Jack Hayford, *The Reward of Worship: The Joy of Fellowship with a Personal God* (Chosen Books, 2007).